June 1973

To Myu
With
from

The FRIENDSHIP BOOK

of FRANCIS GAY

D. C. THOMSON & CO., LTD.
London Glasgow Manchester Dundee

A Thought
For Each Day
In 1973.

I'll take my friends the way they come
            I like 'em when they show the scars,
The wear and tear of battles fought
            The blessed vision of the stars.

EDNA JAQUES

MEN OF THE SEA

Calm and blue the sea today,
Seamen three.
With the tide you'll sail away
Out to sea,
Drifting gently o'er the deep,
Breathing gently in its sleep.

DAVID HOPE

A LESSON IN LOVING

> How wonderful if we could see
> A world of sweet tranquillity,
> Where man no longer warred with man,
> But worked toward a peaceful plan;
> Where each to help the other strove,
> And all were bound in common love.
>
> DAVID HOPE

* Squeakie, the cat, is bringing up these three West Highland terrier pups.

JANUARY

Monday—January 1.

HERE'S a grand thought to carry into a New Year. It was sent to me by a senior citizen who signs herself simply " Granny D."

I'd like to be the sort of friend that you have been to me,
I'd like to be the help that you are always glad to be;
I'd like to mean as much to you, each minute of the day
As you have meant, good friend of mine, to me along the way.
I'm wishing at this special time that I could but repay
A portion of the gladness that you've strewn along my way.
If I could have a single wish, this only would it be—
I'd like to be the sort of friend that you have been to me.

Tuesday—January 2.

IT'S a long time since I had afternoon tea with Sir Harry Lauder at Lauder Ha'. Sir Harry told one funny story after another then, suddenly serious, he said, " Laddie, all of us have our troubles and disappointments." I knew he had had his. " But you know, looking at life as a whole, there are very few ills worth worrying over for more than five minutes."

I have often thought of those words. They have challenged me to keep my troubles in perspective.

THE FRIENDSHIP BOOK

WEDNESDAY—JANUARY 3.

MANY a famous man has found,
  When he has gained the top,
That someone pushed him from below—
  Yes, pushed—and wouldn't stop.
That greatness of his splendid life
Was really fashioned by his wife.

THURSDAY—JANUARY 4.

HAVE you heard of this lovely old tradition? As you know, the true shepherd puts the care and safety of his flock before almost anything else. Often, it means climbing high into the hills, going out into the worst weather, even risking his life for his sheep. And I am told in some places when a shepherd dies, a unique tribute is paid to him. Before he is laid to rest, a wisp of wool is clipped from one of his sheep and placed on his coffin, to be buried with him. It is meant to show his Maker that he, too, was a shepherd, knew the peace of the green hills, the joy of finding the lost sheep, and the quiet pride of counting his flock and finding none missing.

But the wool is intended to say something more. Many a shepherd finds it hard to be in the church as regularly as he might like, for on Sunday morning he may find himself in some remote glen with his sheep. So the wool is to explain simply, " This man was a shepherd, Lord—if you missed him on a Sunday from his place in church, you're sure to understand . . ."

When a king is borne to his rest, his sceptre is laid on his coffin. When a soldier dies, his country's flag adorns his casket. But in its way, that wisp of wool is surely as splendid—and fitting—a tribute as any.

THE FRIENDSHIP BOOK

FRIDAY—JANUARY 5.

I PASS this challenging thought to you—an idea which some of us who feel important and think we are more or less running the whole world may be wise to ponder:

I missed you this morning, Lord.
You were there.
I wasn't.
I was too busy too soon.

SATURDAY—JANUARY 6.

A FEW of us happened to get together one evening recently, and the conversation drifted to a man we all of us knew. We had read that he had gone bankrupt. One member, and one member only, of our little group blamed the bankrupt, and indeed went on to pull him to pieces. The rest were tolerant and understanding.

That, I think is as it should be, first because somebody's misfortune should be regarded as an unhappy affair whether he or she is very greatly to blame or very greatly to be pitied. Secondly: because we know only part of the story we can never be sure we are in a position to judge rightly.

And there comes to mind that old, old poem which has the lines:

Never find fault with the man who limps
 Or stumbles along the road,
Unless you have worn the shoes he wears,
 Or struggled beneath his load.

SUNDAY—JANUARY 7.

A MAN that hath friends must shew himself friendly.

THE FRIENDSHIP BOOK

Monday—January 8.

DR NORMAN MACLEAN in his book, "Set Free," gives this amusing account of a Highland baptism. The precentor's fourth child was to be baptised, and as his third child had almost brought the roof down with her shrieks when the water was sprinkled on, he was rather worried.

On the day of the baptism, however, all went well. The baby cooed gently as the water was sprinkled and he received the name Norman.

Later, Dr Maclean congratulated the precentor on the child's behaviour. "Yes, I was proud of him after the exhibition last year. But I took every possible precaution this time. First, I named him after yourself, for a child called after a minister is bound to behave well and be a credit not only to his parents but to his reverend namesake.

"And in the second place, I myself baptised him every night for a fortnight beforehand, until at last when I sprinkled him he cooed and smiled just as he did in church. This child is full of promise. He learned his first lesson perfectly. He will be a credit to us all!"

Tuesday—January 9.

THE teacher of a class of small boys in a North of England school was amused when her class were asked to draw various shapes in accordance with instructions on the blackboard.

For quite a time there was silence in the classroom except for a low buzz of anxious conversation. Noticing one group of four scratching their heads, the teacher asked, "Can I help?"

Their spokesman at once replied, "No thanks, Miss. Us likes worrying things out us selves."

That's the spirit!

THE FRIENDSHIP BOOK

WEDNESDAY—JANUARY 10.

IN a general way, I like people who are spontaneous and impulsive.

For all that, I must confess it's safer to look before you leap. I have just heard of a kindly woman—by no means well off—who, in a hectic Christmas rush, made a last gallant attempt to catch herself up. Seeing a box of 50 identical greeting cards in a crowded shop, she snapped it up, carried it home, and wrote 49 cards before midnight. She posted the lot next morning, and heaved a sigh of relief.

Later in the day she read her one remaining Christmas card, and was simply horrified at the message:

This little card is just to say
A gift from me is on the way.

As I say, I like warm-hearted, impulsive people —but even they should look before they leap!

THURSDAY—JANUARY 11.

TAKE these lines to heart.

There could be no better time for doing so than the beginning of a year:

I dreamt death came to me one night,
  And Heaven's gates flew wide.
With kindly grace St Peter came,
  And ushered me inside.
There — to my great astonishment —
  Were friends I'd known on earth;
Some I had labelled as unfit,
  And some of little worth.
Indignant words flew to my lips,
  Words I could not set free,
For every face showed stunned surprise . . .
  No one expected me!

THE FRIENDSHIP BOOK

FRIDAY—JANUARY 12.

I WALKED down the street with A. this morning and while we strolled along he told me all about his plans for the future. They sound very good plans—original and ambitious—and his voice rang with enthusiasm as he talked about them. So you will be surprised to learn that I was listening with only half an ear.

You see, I've heard them all before—many times. He's been talking about them for years, but although there seems to be nothing to stop him, he never takes a step nearer putting them into action.

Dreams and plans are fine. But there's a time for dreaming—and a time for doing.

SATURDAY—JANUARY 13.

I SAW them in the park—Geraldine and the tall man. Sunday after Sunday, winter or summer, I have seen Geraldine, now six—she and her father meant everything to each other, the more so because Mum is an invalid who is housebound.

Usually I stop and have a word with them, but one Sunday I deliberately avoided them, turning into a side path. It was Geraldine I had seen from a distance, but the tall man holding her hand was not her father. I knew he had been killed in a car pile-up while travelling on the M1 during fog.

What a tragedy that was, and is—the invalid wife a widow, the wee girl without her father's hand to hold. Uncle Jim, the tall man in the park, is kindness itself, but Daddy has gone for ever, taking the sunshine with him. It is all heartbreaking —and, less than bravely, perhaps, I avoided meeting them because frankly, I did not know what to say.

If only drivers on the M1 that day had gone more slowly in the fog . . .

THE FRIENDSHIP BOOK

SUNDAY—JANUARY 14.

THE Lord shall be a refuge for the oppressed, a shelter in times of trouble. The troubles of my heart are enlarged : O bring me out of my distresses.

MONDAY—JANUARY 15.

THE edict had gone forth—any soldier failing to keep the night watch would be shot.

Napoleon had issued the order, and he himself toured part of the camp. At midnight he found a sentry asleep. Well, that was unpardonable—but the General stood by ; and when the sentry, wearied after the day's march, woke from his nap, his superior said gently : " Don't worry, man. I kept guard for you."

Punishments are needed . . . but it is still true, that if you can show mercy or smile away a little misdemeanour, or forgive a word said in temper—well, you are doing a lovely and a worthwhile thing.

TUESDAY—JANUARY 16.

I DO not know his name, but I am told that in the Borders there is a man who delights to go off with his camera " shooting " people—people in towns or villages, in fields or coming out of church or looking over a bridge or taking a child a walk . . . And this young man talks to the people he photographs in colour, and then sends his snap to friends who are housebound, sending also a typescript account of his adventures and of what he heard.

It seems to me a very happy hobby ; and I feel that some of us might do worse than tramp the countryside looking for and talking to interesting people !

THE FRIENDSHIP BOOK

WEDNESDAY—JANUARY 17.

I HAD a little hammer once
   With which I used to strike.
I went a-knocking everywhere
   At folk I didn't like.
I knocked most everybody, but
   I found it didn't pay,
For when they saw me coming
   They went the other way.

THURSDAY—JANUARY 18.

ONE of the most remarkable letters I've ever received came from George Jackson, and it tells me about life in the eventide home in Abbey Road, Barrow. The amazing thing is that George has been completely blind for many years!

I won't pretend the writing is copperplate, but I am able to read every word, and I don't mind admitting it's a great deal more legible than my own writing much of the time.

The secret, believe it or not, lies in a length of elastic. All his life, George was a keen letter writer, until he lost his sight. It meant he'd to depend on someone else to write his letters, and that just wasn't the same. When he moved into Ostley House, the matron saw how much he yearned to be able to write. So she brought him a board criss-crossed with horizontal lengths of elastic, about half an inch apart. Then she slipped a piece of paper beneath the elastic lines, and handed George a pen.

The elastic lines guide his pen, and though George could not see what he had written, the matron assured him every word was clear.

And I'm proud that one of his first letters was to me, telling me the great news.

PEAT

As the scent of the peat-fire fills the air
   And the peat-flames flicker and glow,
I think I can see in their dancing
   Faces from long ago
Of the people before me who tilled this earth
And sang their songs by my peat-fire hearth.

DAVID HOPE

A SECRET BAY

We all have dreams of such a peaceful bay,
Sheltered and warm, far from the busy throng;
Where we can pass the lazy hours away,
Basking in sea and sun the whole day long.

DAVID HOPE

THE FRIENDSHIP BOOK

FRIDAY—JANUARY 19.

I LIKE the story of the minister who, though in a hurry himself, stopped his car to give a lift to two men going his way.

To make up for the delay, he increased speed. Only he forgot to slow down going through a town and was caught for speeding.

Very much worried, he felt ashamed that he, a minister, should be reported for breaking the law.

But when he set the two men down, they said, "Don't worry, Reverend, about being caught for speeding. You see, we're just out of prison. We're pickpockets and we pinched the policeman's notebook. You'll hear no more of the charge!"

Dishonest? Certainly. But they were doing their best to help!

SATURDAY—JANUARY 20.

SOCRATES, the famous Greek philosopher who lived four centuries before Christ, was one of the clearest thinkers of all time. He had also a gallant and whimsical spirit.

Condemned to death because of his plain speaking, he was compelled to drink a cup of poison. A moment before he died, and while his friends looked on and wept, the condemned man remained unbelievably cheery. One of his companions asked: "Where shall we bury you?"

Even then Socrates held to his faith, and peppered it with a rare wit. Lightly he replied: "Anywhere you like . . . *if you can catch me!*"

SUNDAY—JANUARY 21.

EXCEPT the Lord build the house, they labour in vain that build it.

THE FRIENDSHIP BOOK

Monday—January 22.

I HEARD last Christmas of a little girl—member of a Sunday school class—who was upset while with a small group delivering gifts on Christmas Eve. After knocking at a door, they were admitted into a room where an old lady, with a shawl round her thin shoulders, listened to what they had to say, thanked them for their little gifts, and asked them to sing " Still the Night."

" And when we'd finished," said the little girl, " she just cried and cried . . and we thought we'd been kind!"

I feel sure you'll understand, if the young lass didn't.

Tuesday—January 23.

I KNOW a family of five which is remarkably closely knit.

There are the parents, and one girl and two boys, all three in their twenties. The two boys are a hundred miles from home, the girl lives fifty miles away, but there is never a week-end when either one, two or three of them are not at home—and glad to be with their parents and each other.

In these days such a thing is less common than formerly; and I think these homing young folk are what they are because as children Mum and Dad never made them feel they were unwanted, and always did things together with their children. It seems now to be paying off handsome dividends.

Wednesday—January 24.

TEN-SECOND sermon with a smile:
It wasn't raining when Noah built the Ark.

THE FRIENDSHIP BOOK

THURSDAY—JANUARY 25.

TONIGHT, Burns Nichts will be held all over the land.

At many, his famous poem "To a Mouse" will be spoken. But I'd like to tell you of another mouse. The story begins when a young artist went to a newspaper editor in Kansas to ask for a job. He was turned down. He was told he had no talent.

One day, as he sat despondently at his drawing-board in his father's garage, a mouse crept out of a hole in the floor and scurried towards him. He sat smiling at its antics. Next day, it ventured nearer. Soon it sat on his easel as he worked, eating the crumbs he'd brought.

Then, once more, the young man tried to make his way in the world. Again, failure. As he sat despairing in a cheap boarding-house, he remembered the friendly mouse. Dejectedly he picked up his pencil and, to pass the time, began to sketch it. That was the start of one of the greatest success stories of all time. For the young artist was Walt Disney, and the sketches became Mickey Mouse.

As a poor farmer Burns gave us poems that go round the world. As a penniless failure, Walt Disney created a magic world that has brought laughter and delight to millions.

How true that the darkest hour comes just before the dawn.

FRIDAY—JANUARY 26.

WHEN daylight's scarce and, what is worse,
  The chilly nights are long;
Though toes are cold and we feel old,
  And lots of things are wrong;
We'll somehow keep on keeping on,
Till bitter days and nights are gone!

THE FRIENDSHIP BOOK

SATURDAY—JANUARY 27.

THIS message, found in a church magazine in Vancouver, surely holds as much for folk here as it does on the other side of the Atlantic.

Hold this square to your face and blow on it.
If it turns green, call your doctor.
If it turns brown, see your dentist.
If it turns purple, see a psychiatrist.
If it turns red, visit your banker.
If it turns black, make your will.

If it stays the same colour, you're in first-class health and there's no reason on earth why you shouldn't be in church next Sunday morning!

Not to be taken too seriously, of course. But just enough of a rebuke, perhaps, to do the trick!

SUNDAY—JANUARY 28.

EYE hath not seen, nor ear heard, neither have entered into the heart of man, the things which God hath prepared for them that love Him.

MONDAY—JANUARY 29.

WE read in the Gospel of St John (chapter 3, verse 16) that God so loved the world . . .

Come to think of it, what a world to love : cruel then (as now), full of fanatics and thieves and murderers and toiling millions and groaning slaves and miserable beggars and suffering men, women and children . . . yet, according to our faith, God loved all these. It seems unbelievable, but, of course, we know it to be true.

And, as the old hymn has it: "We must love Him, too."

That's the only way to a new and a better world. And you and I know it.

THE FRIENDSHIP BOOK

TUESDAY—JANUARY 30.

TWO of the most charming folk we know are Ian and Moira—getting on but full of the zest for living! They have been married forty years, and Ian was telling me the other day that for over thirty-nine of those years they've never had even a little quarrel! Sounds unbelievable.

But they fell out in their first year together. Ian was on his way to becoming a bank manager—a precise, careful man. Moira was lovely, energetic, fond of outdoor games, a wonderful cook, the perfect hostess . . . but just couldn't be tidy! There were newspapers and magazines scattered around the spotless house. If she came in after a game or a visit her shoes would be on the stairs and a glove by the sink and her parcels everywhere and her handbag on a chair . . . And Ian didn't like that. He said so. Moira resented it. They went for each other.

Then all the in-fighting ceased. Why? Because it had occurred to Ian that he had a wife in a million, a loving and lovely wife with only one weakness. Why let that wreck their marriage? So he began saying nothing about this and that out of place, but just went round the house picking up things and putting them where they belonged.

Just that. Nothing more. Is Ian a spineless cissie or a very clever man? I wonder.

WEDNESDAY—JANUARY 31.

TO help or bless the whole wide world
  Is far too much for me,
But in my little sphere I'll try
  A gentle friend to be.
And at the last I may well find
I've comforted by being kind.

FEBRUARY

THURSDAY—FEBRUARY 1.

I HAVE the impression that folk today are inclined to be discontented whether they have much or little. It's a pity, for happiness is more or less independent of wealth or poverty, good times or bad. Fiddler Jones was happy. Edgar Lee Masters, the American poet, wrote of him. He spent his time making music for others, and he ended his life with "forty acres, a broken fiddle . . . *and not a single regret.*"

Forty acres are not much. A broken fiddle is useless. But to have made a lot of people happy, and to have died with not even one regret . . . wasn't this magnificent?

FRIDAY—FEBRUARY 2.

THIS little story is about a teenager, who, in a moment of stress and bewilderment, declared she was leaving home for ever. There and then she stormed out, taking with her nothing, not even a coat or a few shillings.

All afternoon she walked — mile after mile in city streets, getting nowhere, becoming tired, also hungry, and feeling more foolish every minute. At last, she turned into a small coffee bar, ordered a hot drink and decided to tell the proprietor she had no money—she didn't care what happened.

Suddenly, somebody sat down at the little table — her father. "What about another cup?" he asked gently.

That was enough. All anger gone, the young lass was only too glad to return to the home where, as she'd known all along, she was dearly loved.

It's difficult to run away from a love that follows.

THE FRIENDSHIP BOOK

SATURDAY—FEBRUARY 3.

I THINK I'll treat myself. Why not?
Since flowers I adore.
I'll buy a pretty bunch or two . . .
I might buy even more.
And just for fun this clear, bright day,
I'll give each lovely bunch away!

SUNDAY—FEBRUARY 4.

THE fool hath said in his heart, There is no God.

MONDAY—FEBRUARY 5.

A POLICEMAN was striding to the scene—a boy had fallen off his cycle, or so an elderly man told me. But a girl said he'd been knocked down by a motorist, and a postman chipped in with, " No, a woman stepped off the pavement right into him."

The boy, who seemed more confused than hurt, had already picked himself up, and I heard him saying his chain had come off, causing him to swerve suddenly.

The little crowd melted away, and I hurried on. But I thought to myself, " I shall not attempt to become a historian."

Who, I wonder, would like to write the history of their town during the last ten years, or an account of events in Northern Ireland during the last twelve months? Where would you get the truth, the significant reasons and grievances, let alone details of who did this or that? And when it comes to the history of last century or the days of the first Queen Elizabeth, how can a historian disentangle the details?

If there was confusion over such a small happening, I'll leave it to others to write our history!

THE FRIENDSHIP BOOK

Tuesday—February 6.

FROM Prince Edward Island, Canada, comes this rhyme, which expresses a bit of homely philosophy:

One step won't get you very far—
  You've got to keep on walking.
One word won't tell folks who you are—
  You've got to keep on talking.
One foot won't make you very tall—
  You've got to keep on growing.
One trip to church won't tell you all—
  You've got to keep on going!

Wednesday—February 7.

I MET a friend the other day who asked if I'd heard about Ian. I said, "No. Nothing wrong, I hope—don't tell me he's been made redundant."

"No need to worry," he replied. "Ian's been promoted. I thought maybe you'd like to congratulate him."

All that was very pleasant; but I had the feeling that my friend spoilt things a bit by adding, "Oh, well, I suppose he deserves it . . . Anyhow, he's lucky!"

As it happens, I've known Ian quite a while; and—between you and me—Ian hasn't been promoted because he's lucky. He's been promoted because he's earned it, and will be useful in his higher capacity.

Undoubtedly these things *do* come by what seems sheer good luck, but I have noticed that most of the lucky people I've known have worked hard and long, have put thought and energy into their job . . . and calling such folk lucky is—well, less than fair.

Don't you agree?

THE FRIENDSHIP BOOK

THURSDAY—FEBRUARY 8.

WE come to your window each day—
  It's hunger that makes us so bold.
We're hungry, so hungry, dear folks,
  And, oh, we're so terribly cold.
If only some crumbs you will fling,
We'll thank you by singing in spring!

FRIDAY—FEBRUARY 9.

SOME years ago, Annie McKenzie had a stroke. Though she managed to pull through, her right side was paralysed. She'd always written with her right hand. Now she couldn't even hold a pen.

How true it is you never miss a familiar thing till you lose it, and that's what Annie found about losing the power to write. She couldn't leave a note for the milkman, copy a recipe, write a Christmas card or even fill in her pension forms.

Yet since then I've received a beautifully-written letter from Annie and every word penned with her left hand! Yes, before she left hospital she'd been taught to write again, at nearly 70. It meant a lot of practice and hard work from Annie, and much patience from those teaching her. But how grateful she is for the full use of her other hand.

That's therapy. Yet I once thought it a cold word. How wrong can you be!

SATURDAY—FEBRUARY 10.

WHEN you send a letter,
  Pause before you write.
Don't dwell on your troubles—
  Think up something bright.
Send your love—and, by and by,
You'll receive a nice reply.

THE FRIENDSHIP BOOK

Sunday—February 11.

He that is of a merry heart hath a continual feast.

Monday—February 12.

It was a great day when young Bobby Brown was told he could learn to play the bagpipes.

His uncles were grand pipers, and there was no keener pupil in the Highlands.

But someone else was just as keen—Bobby's sister, Bessie. From the age of six, Bessie had been unable to walk because of polio and she couldn't move an inch without a wheelchair. So when Bob came in from his piping lesson, he'd show her what he'd been taught, and in the long hours of sitting alone in her chair, Bessie would take up her brother's pipes and try to master the intricacies of rhythm and fingering.

Well, Bob became one of the finest pipers in the land. Indeed, he was chosen as the Queen's piper and, until he retired not long ago, it was his privilege to play every morning at Balmoral. But Bessie, too, became famous, even from her wheelchair. She is recognised as one of Deeside's best teachers of piping and many a young lad owes all his skill to what he has learned from Bessie. Not only that, for many years Bessie was a well-known judge of piping and today, nearing seventy, she still travels all over Scotland from her home in Banchory, where she lives alone, to hear youngsters match their skill against one another.

Yes, it was a great day for young Bobby Brown when his father said he could learn the pipes. But perhaps it turned out to be an even greater day for his sister, for whom it was the gateway to a new life.

THE FRIENDSHIP BOOK

TUESDAY—FEBRUARY 13.

RECENTLY a friend passed on to me this wish, and I feel I must pass it on to you, hoping that you may pass it on to someone else, especially someone who is finding the journey of life less than easy:

Here's wishing you—
Peace for the pathway,
Wisdom for the work,
Friends for the fireside,
Love to the last.

WEDNESDAY—FEBRUARY 14.

"OUT of the mouths of babes and sucklings" they say, and it's true how often, unwittingly, children utter profound truths.

Like the farmer's schoolboy son who was particularly interested in the 23rd Psalm—the Shepherd Psalm, as it is so often called. One Sunday he asked his Sunday school teacher if Eastern shepherds had dogs to help them.

The teacher had to confess that she did not know the answer, but promised to find out, if she could.

The following Sunday the bright boy was too quick for her. Before she could mention the Psalm, he told her eagerly, "I've found out about the dogs myself, Miss. Eastern farmers *did* have them; and the writer of the 23rd Psalm had two. What's more, Miss, I know their names, because it says in the Bible: *Goodness and Mercy shall follow me.*"

Deeply touched, the teacher went to her minister and told him what the lad had said. Then, hesitantly, she added, "But I think he's wrong. The shepherd in the Bible had actually three dogs—and the name of the third was Surely."

THURSDAY—FEBRUARY 15.

I DON'T know who wrote this little verse, but it's a must for all Dads.

There are little eyes upon you and they're watching night and day;
There are little ears that quickly take in every word you say;
There are little hands all eager to do everything you do
And a little boy who's dreaming of the day he'll be like you.
You're the little fellow's idol, you're the wisest of the wise;
In his little mind about you no suspicions ever rise.
There's a wide-eyed little fellow who believes you're always right
And his ears are always open and he watches day and night.
You are setting an example every day in all you do
For the little boy who's waiting to grow up to be like you.

FRIDAY—FEBRUARY 16.

MRS BETTY WALLACE was at her niece's wedding recently.

She wrote to tell me all about the great day, adding that the minister told some good stories. Among them the tale of the parson who called on a member, and mentioned he hadn't seen her in church recently.

"No," she said, "It's been awfully wet lately." The minister smiled. "But, Miss Smith," he reminded her, "it's dry in the kirk."

"Too true," retorted Miss Smith, "especially the sermons!"

THE FRIENDSHIP BOOK

SATURDAY—FEBRUARY 17.

I EXPECT you've had them on your doorstep . . . the smiling evangelists, usually quite young, hoping to win new converts to their faith.

I heard about an elderly body who opened the door to a smiling stranger the other day. She knew the evangelists were in the area, but she didn't expect to find one wearing overalls and a flat cap. But what else could he be, when his first question was, " Excuse me, but are you converted ?"

" Thank you," said granny firmly. " But I'm quite happy with my present church."

The visitor's smile broadened. " No, ma'am," he explained. " I'm from the Gas Board — to convert you to natural gas !"

SUNDAY—FEBRUARY 18.

JUDGE me, O Lord, according to my righteousness, and according to mine integrity that is in me.

MONDAY—FEBRUARY 19.

THE Lady of the House and I may as well come clean. We do our fair share of grumbling.

Such a lot seems wrong these days. Almost everywhere you turn things are bad, at home and abroad. On top of world problems, there are the little things like the grocery bill which added up wrongly to the tune of 60 new pence, and the local plumber who said three weeks ago, " I'll be round first thing tomorrow," and who is still coming.

We're rather ashamed of all our grumbling. After all, we know fine that in a few years' time we shall be looking back on this present year, and referring to it as the good old days !

THE FRIENDSHIP BOOK

TUESDAY—FEBRUARY 20.

I KNOW not how or why I'm here,
I know not whence I came.
I only know that while I'm here
I ought to play the game,
And serve and bless, each friendly day,
All other folk who tread my way.

WEDNESDAY—FEBRUARY 21.

DID I ever tell you about the organist who, some years ago, as a result of a bad accident was compelled to have his left hand amputated? The physical ordeal was bad enough, but when he looked at the unsightly stump, he knew that he could never play the organ again—and music was his life.

One day a friend invited him to take a walk, and the two turned into the church where the organist had played so magnificently. "You sit here," the friend suggested, pointing to a seat in the nave, "and I'll play to you."

The musician was hurt that his friend should be so thoughtlessly cruel, but for all that, he listened to the music being played. Then he left the pew and walked to the organ console. To his astonishment his friend had his left arm in a sling and was playing with his right hand only and his feet on the pedals.

Smiling, the friend gently explained his trick: "For months I've been experimenting and practising, and I find I can do remarkably well with one hand and my feet. If I can, so can you. It will take time, but it's amazing what you can do if you keep on trying."

So life for a musician with only one hand became well worthwhile.

THE FRIENDSHIP BOOK

THURSDAY—FEBRUARY 22.

MRS RILEY, 102 Dundad Street, Stockton-on-Tees, is a widow now. But she treasures the memories of forty happy years with her husband, and believes that if more wives followed the twelve golden rules which she always kept, fewer marriages might run into difficulties.

When you marry him, love him ;
After you marry him, study him ;
If he's secretive, trust him ;
If he's sad, cheer him ;
When he's talkative, listen to him ;
When he's quarrelsome, ignore him ;
If he's jealous, cure him ;
If he cares naught for pleasure, coax him ;
If he favours society, accompany him ;
When he deserves it, kiss him ;
Let him know how well you understand him ;
But never let him realise that you manage him !

FRIDAY—FEBRUARY 23.

THERE'S a challenge in this story.

It's about a little boy in a school in the East End of London. One day he asked his mother if he could ask a school friend home to tea.

As there's a mixture of races in this school, Mum hesitated. " Is he a coloured boy ?" she asked.

Her small son considered. " I don't know," he replied. " But I'll find out tomorrow."

It seems to me this is a reminder that children are children the world over, and that they simply do not notice what colour other children are—brown, white, red, black, all are one, and all are willing to play with each other and be friends.

So where does race prejudice begin ?

Makes you think, doesn't it ?

THE FRIENDSHIP BOOK

SATURDAY—FEBRUARY 24.

GRANNIES, as a rule, can teach us something worth learning.

Not long ago Miss Jean Devine, 2 Victoria Road, St Annes, told me her grandmother passed to her rest recently aged 97. Grannie believed firmly in most of the old-fashioned virtues—especially prayer. And after remembering others, last of all she would pray for herself, in these words:

God, give me sympathy and sense,
*   Help me to keep my courage high;*
Give to me calm and confidence—
*   And please, a twinkle in my eye!*

All simple things—but Grannie knew they add up to the secret of successful living.

SUNDAY—FEBRUARY 25.

CAST Thy burden upon the Lord, and He shall sustain thee.

MONDAY—FEBRUARY 26.

A FRIEND remarked the other day that some of the smallest men he had known had been over six-foot in their socks.

Perhaps I looked surprised, for he went on to explain, "After all, a man can be big in stature and yet very small in spirit, can't he?"

My friend's joke reminded me of the ranchers in America who asked the superintendent of a mission many miles off if they could have a minister.

"How big a man do you want?" the superintendent asked.

"Well," was the magnificent reply, "we're not very particular, but when he's on his knees we'd like to have him reach Heaven."

DREAM COTTAGE

So there you are, dear cottage,
Sitting companionably beside the river,
Off the road from somewhere and down the winding lane.
The daffodils nod their greeting as I come
Past the bridge to nowhere.
Your gate creaks, I remember,
The old oak door stands comfortably ajar,
As down the garden path you come to greet me.

DAVID HOPE

OLD DURHAM

"*Half church of God, half castle 'gainst the Scots,*"
So ran the phrase of Durham long ago.
In softer days old Durham still stands guard
O'er roof and wall and labouring folk below.

To church of God folk turned in dire need,
The stubborn walls their screen in danger's hour;
Long gone the foe, but humble souls may find
Within these walls a still more mighty power.

DAVID HOPE

NEWS!

Blazing a trail across the fields,
They raise their trumpets high,
Persuading unbelievers
That better days are nigh.
Year by year their news they bring,
These golden heralds of the spring.

DAVID HOPE

THE FRIENDSHIP BOOK

TUESDAY—FEBRUARY 27.

DURING the war there were, all over the country, groups of women who met together to knit for the soldiers. They made up parcels of woollies, and often put a little text or friendly message in the thumb of a glove or the toe of a sock. One mother, knitting at her local W.V.S. centre, put a stamp-sized card in a sock with the words — FEAR NOT.

At the London H.Q., the socks were bundled into a large parcel for troops in Holland; and that one pair of socks happened to be dished out to a soldier who was terribly depressed and was scared of the impending attack.

He found the card saying FEAR NOT, and read the initials of the sender—they were the same as his mother's, and although he was sure it could only be coincidence, he still felt that somehow the message was meant especially for him.

Well, believe it or not, he eventually learned that the message had indeed come from his mother. Marvellous, isn't it, how somehow her love had reached out and given her son the courage he needed for the offensive, an ordeal which he came through unscathed.

WEDNESDAY—FEBRUARY 28.

HERE'S a smile to end the month with.

Years ago, Dr Charles Spurgeon, the famous preacher, was asked if, in his opinion, a man who played the trumpet on Sunday would ever go to Heaven.

Spurgeon thought for a moment. Then he smiled. " I don't see why not," he replied. " But I doubt if the man next door to him ever would!"

MARCH

Thursday—March 1.

A GOOD, loving mother is one of the most wonderful blessings God has given. She lives to give. She is happy to sacrifice, if need be. She is always busy doing little things to make her children happy—and if they grow up to be honest and true and useful and kind, her heart is thrilled. Nothing moves her more deeply and gratefully. A good mother finds all her happiness in her family, and she lives only to serve.

The Jews are aware of this, perhaps more than any other race on earth. And in their Talmud are these lovely and challenging words:

God could not be everywhere, so he made mothers.

Friday—March 2.

I HEARD the other day of a small boy who had been saving coppers for months so that he could give a pound to a church effort which had captured his imagination. At last he had amassed a whole pound and took his precious box to the minister, who counted out the coins. Just at the end of the operation one of the smallest coins slipped between his fingers, rolled across the floor and vanished in a crack near the wall. " Oh," wailed the child, " now my pound *isn't* a pound !"

The boy was a perfectionist. Some of us have allowed our sights to be lowered—if a thing is fairly well done, it'll do. But that's a poor way of living, isn't it?

I will not preach. I will just remind you again of the little fellow who wailed, " Now my pound *isn't* a pound !" And it wasn't!

THE FRIENDSHIP BOOK

SATURDAY—MARCH 3.

NOT long ago Miss Margaret Black saw a shop window display of colourful cards for Father's Day. All very well, she thought, for those who are fathers. What's more, mothers have Mother's Day, grannies have Grannie's Day — there's even a Grandpa's Day!

But what of all those who, like herself, have never married? They don't get special cards—and, surely, in many cases they're the very ones whose lives are in most need of brightening up.

So Margaret, a pensioner herself, announced to all her friends that she was to set aside September 25 as Maiden Day, for all " unclaimed treasures "; otherwise known, she adds, as old maids or spinsters! She bought a selection of cards and sent them to any unclaimed treasures she knew.

And what do you think? When the postie stopped at Margaret's door he brought no fewer than fourteen cards for her!

Maybe there are getting to be too many of these special days. But maybe, like the Lady of the House and I, you feel Unclaimed Treasures' Day is one that deserves to catch on.

SUNDAY—MARCH 4.

THE Lord is my strength and my shield; my heart trusted in Him, and I am helped.

MONDAY—MARCH 5.

MANY people have tried to define a woman's intuition, but none has succeeded quite so well, I think, as the friend who put it thus:
Intuition is what enables a woman to contradict her husband before he says a word!

THE FRIENDSHIP BOOK

TUESDAY—MARCH 6.

THE postman delivered quite a few cards for Susan's third birthday, but one of her favourites came from her father. It wished her a happy birthday, and the verse said:

Little girls are very sweet
And very precious, too.
That's why this card is being sent
With lots of love to you.

Lovely words, sent to a lovely toddler by her dad, who waited nine years for a daughter, and, just over a year later, was blessed with a son, too. Yet perhaps I had better tell you that a few months ago Susan's dad cleared out and went to live with another woman. Since then he hasn't seen his children. They and their mother don't even know where he is.

Even as Susan clutched the card with its empty mockery of a message, she was asking her mum why Daddy left home . . . does he not love us now . . . will we ever see him again? All Mummy could do was hug her little girl, fight back the tears, and wonder if life could ever hold any happiness for them again.

I wish there was some way I could tell Susan's dad that he has thrown away one of life's most precious blessings, and that one day he may realise what he has lost.

WEDNESDAY—MARCH 7.

MOST everything for months and months,
 No matter what you do,
Has somehow gone as wrong as wrong—
 It's quite unnerving you.
No panic now! With all your might,
Hold on, hold on, till things go right.

THE FRIENDSHIP BOOK

Thursday—March 8.

DOG-LOVERS will, I think, like this dog's prayer written by Piero Scanziani:

Lord of all creatures, make the man who is my master as faithful to others as I am to him. Cause him to love his family and friends as much as I love him. May he be the guardian of his blessings as I guard him and his possessions.

When I wag my tail, Lord, may he have a ready smile and be as grateful as I am quick to lick his hand. Grant him my patience. Teach him to wait without complaining as I wait for his return. Give him my courage. Keep for him the youthfulness of my heart and the cheerfulness of my thoughts.

Lord of all creatures, as I am always truly a dog, grant that my master may always truly be a man.

Friday—March 9.

MY old friend John Robertson is seldom able to leave his bed.

But when I called to see him, he had an Ordnance Survey map of the Western Highlands spread out before him. " On your travels ? " I quipped.

John's face creased into a gallant smile, and the pale blue eyes twinkled. "Aye," he said, lying back as if tired, " it's been a strenuous journey. First, I'd to climb Ben More, and then travel via Killichronan to Tobermory, and away to the island of Eigg, where I ran into bad weather, but oh, what a sunset after a storm . . ."

I doubt if John will ever climb even a little hill again or ever set eyes on Coll or Canna, but how courageously he turns his enforced rest to good account, and with a map and a brave spirit roams the mountains and glens and islands he knows so well and loves so much !

THE FRIENDSHIP BOOK

SATURDAY—MARCH 10.

IF you'd to choose between being deaf or blind, would you rather lose your sight or your hearing?

Surely there isn't a more difficult question to answer. Whether to give up seeing the faces of loved ones, a rainbow or the joyful splash of a new pair of curtains, and grope your way through a life of darkness; or to lose for ever the sounds we take so much for granted . . . voices, music, the song of birds, the laughter of children.

Not long ago I was speaking to the Rev. O. Laird White, of Aberdeen, who is chaplain to the deaf all over the North of Scotland. He told me he asked 39 men and women who were both deaf and blind to say whether they would rather see or hear again.

To his surprise, no fewer than 38 of them said without a moment's hesitation that they considered deafness to be the greater handicap, and that they would willingly remain blind if they could only hear again. Mr White wondered why this should be. All 38 gave much the same answer—that while blindness cuts you off from things, deafness cuts you off from people.

Perhaps, for those of us blessed with both sight and hearing, it is easier to sympathise with the blind, for it is easier to imagine the handicap it would be to us. I think this story helps us to understand how much of a shadow a world of silence can also cast on life.

SUNDAY—MARCH 11.

SHEW Thy marvellous loving kindness, O Thou that savest by Thy right hand them which put their trust in Thee from those that rise up against them.

THE FRIENDSHIP BOOK

MONDAY—MARCH 12.

*WE bless Thee, Lord, for all this common life
Can give of rest and joy amidst its strife;
For earth and trees and sea and clouds and springs;
For work, and all the lessons that it brings.*

TUESDAY—MARCH 13.

EXCUSE me—but do you covet your neighbour's ox?

The question is prompted by a chat I had with my neighbour. In talking about the state of the world, he'd mentioned to his wife that maybe a bit more of the ten commandments was needed.

"Eleven," corrected Susan, his ten-year-old.

"Ten commandments," said Dad. But Susan dug her heels in. "Eleven," she said, and added her teacher said the first four show us our duty to God, and the next six remind us of our duty to other people.

"Well," said her father, "four and six make ten." Susan smiled. "But there's another," she said. "Our teacher said that in its way it's the most important commandment of all . . . John 13, 34." And off she went.

"D'you know, Francis," her father added, shaking his head, "she's right."

You know where to find it!

WEDNESDAY—MARCH 14.

ONE of my absent-minded colleagues beamed his way home recently wielding a brolly.

"You see, my dear," he announced. "I haven't forgotten to bring my umbrella home this time!"

"H'm," his wife sniffed. "Very thoughtful of you, dear. But you didn't take it with you this morning!"

THE FRIENDSHIP BOOK

THURSDAY—MARCH 15.

SAYING a prayer is actually so simple that most people cannot do it. They have to use high-sounding phrases while all the time the true prayer need not even be spoken.

There was a friend of mine who, years ago, asked God's help in keeping his temper. God did not answer the prayer. At last my friend, distressed because his sharp temper was alienating him from his wife and children, went alone into his bedroom and prayed earnestly: "Lord, make me all over again—a new and better man."

That simple, agonising prayer was answered. He did rise a better man, and ever since that day he has kept the love of wife and family, and though he didn't ask God to mend his temper, he has never once since that day lost it!

Simplicity, whole-hearted surrender, that is the kind of prayer which brings results.

FRIDAY—MARCH 16.

EVER thought of a friend as a lamp?

When you consider the idea you realise the comparison is a good one. After all, we are on a journey. Most of the time most of us find the road rough and the light poor and the way ahead altogether dark.

Well, then, if a friend is a lamp, and a lamp that is alight, he or she helps to make or keep the way we have to tread more easily seen. So keep your friends as long as possible, because—as a friend of mine puts it, quaintly but impressively:

I try to keep them bright by faith
 And never let them dim with doubt
For every time I lose a friend
 A little shining lamp goes out.

BEST OF FRIENDS

*My best friend's Jane, my pony,
And Jane's best friend is me.
We understand each other,
As anyone can see.
I give to Jane the best of care;
She takes me rides to everywhere.*

DAVID HOPE

BEAUTIFUL ONIONS

I love the scent of flowers,
Carnation, stock and rose,
But something in its season eclipses even those.
The onion! Praise it, boiled or fried,
The sauce of hunger satisfied.

DAVID HOPE

THE FRIENDSHIP BOOK

Saturday—March 17.

By the merest chance I happened to come across a book the other day in which I found this short story which is a big challenge to you and to me. Indeed, it made me think all the way home—I felt, somehow, it was a warning to me to live a useful life. And I think that did me good! Here's the anecdote, true or untrue, which (though I found it in a book) is actually carved on a tombstone:

Here, at Stoke-by-Nayland, once lived a wealthy miser who pulled down crows' nests for fuel and got the usual reward of suchlike thrift by having half a million half a minute before he died—and nothing half a minute later.

Sunday—March 18.

Therefore my heart greatly rejoiceth; and with my song will I praise Him.

Monday—March 19.

I have just heard about a little girl of four years who, during a special children's service at church, stood up with the rest of the young folk and, without either hymn book or hymn-sheet (in any case, she couldn't read), sang every verse of every hymn, opening her mouth wide and obviously enjoying herself immensely.

On the way home after the service the child's mother asked how her small daughter had learnt so many hymns off by heart. The little lass chuckled. "Oh," she said happily, "the only hymns I know by heart are *Baa, Baa, Black Sheep* and *Little Boy Blue*, and it was those I kept singing all the time in church!"

THE FRIENDSHIP BOOK

TUESDAY—MARCH 20.

I DON'T know who sent me those lines, but I think you will agree the writer not only possesses a gifted pen, but understands the meaning of true friendship—

It is great to say, " Good-morning!"
It is fine to say, " Hello!"
But better still to grasp the hand
Of a loyal friend you know.
A smile may be forgotten,
A word misunderstood,
But the warm clasp of the human hand
Is the pledge of brotherhood.

WEDNESDAY—MARCH 21.

OVER 200 years ago, a party of important men were discussing short prayers. Sir William Wyndham said the shortest prayer he had ever heard was the prayer of a common soldier, just before the Battle of Blenheim—"O God, if there be a God, save my soul, if I have a soul." The Bishop of Rochester replied:—"Your prayer, Sir William, is indeed very short, but I remember another as short, but much better, offered up likewise by a poor soldier in the same circumstances—" O God, if in the day of battle, I forget thee, do thou not forget me."

THURSDAY—MARCH 22.

I'D like to hand out medals to
 Plain folk who, day by day,
Live unspectacularly but
 Help folk upon their way.
And do it all as if in fun
So's folk don't know until it's done!

THE FRIENDSHIP BOOK

FRIDAY—MARCH 23.

THE famous missionary, Mary Slessor, worked tirelessly for the Africans she loved. This is how she described the kind of assistant she longed for: "women not afraid of work or of filth of any kind, moral or material. Women who can nurse a baby or teach a child to wash and comb as well as to read and write; women who can tactfully smooth over a roughness and, for Christ's sake, bear a snub. If they can play Beethoven and paint and draw and speak French and German, so much the better, but we can want all these latter accomplishments if they have only a loving heart, willing hands and common sense."

There will always be room in this world for people like that.

SATURDAY—MARCH 24.

SOME years ago a cargo vessel in the Pacific became helpless because her steering gear had broken down during a storm. She radioed for help, and the captain of another vessel changed course, and for three days and nights stood by the helpless vessel, unable to do anything till the storm abated and the repair was carried out.

How frustrating to see a friend in need but be unable to help.

We all know the feeling, don't we, when a friend is ill or worried or has suffered a bereavement, and there's nothing we can do except stand-by.

Nothing? Well, just to know that someone *is* standing-by can be such a comfort in times of stress.

SUNDAY—MARCH 25.

IN Thee, O Lord, do I put my trust.

THE FRIENDSHIP BOOK

Monday—March 26.

YOU don't need me to tell you what an incentive is.
It's something to arouse enthusiasm or incite to action; a spur, if you like.

All this, of course, you know. But did you realise the word incentive comes from a Latin word "incentivus," which means "setting the tune"? It has come all the way down the centuries from the days when the conquering Romans sang as they marched, their feet aching, their muscles stiff, longing to lie down and rest—but just by singing as they marched along they somehow kept going. It was much the same in the first World War.

So, remember, singing helps the work along. Whistle while you work. As Sir Harry Lauder used to tell us, singing is the thing to keep you cheery!

Tuesday—March 27.

MOST of us don't need telling (though there's no harm in a reminder) that the Bible is the book of books, "the good Book" which our fathers loved so much because it comforts in sorrow, guides us when perplexed, sets the standard for living and points the road to heaven. We neglect it at our peril.

And I would add that we shall be the poorer if all we do is to read it perfunctorily. The Bible is more than merely a book to read—it is a book to read and think about and act upon.

That is why I pass on a word spoken recently by a Japanese youth who had become a Christian. Talking about his new way of life, he said: "I am now reading my Bible and behaving it."

Good indeed to read your Bible. Better still to live it!

THE FRIENDSHIP BOOK

WEDNESDAY—MARCH 28.

LIFE'S often cruel—this you know—
But if, when you're afraid,
You learn to sing like anything,
You're sure to make the grade.
Self-pity gets you just nowhere,
But courage helps to banish care.

THURSDAY—MARCH 29.

THIS is the secret of two Elizabeths.

One is the Queen Mother. The other is a widow who left this country before the First World War to live in Canada—Mrs Elizabeth Brown, of Wilson Road South, Oshawa, near Toronto.

In 1939 Bessie Brown decided to send the Queen Mother a birthday card. For one thing, Britain was on the brink of war, and she felt the King and Queen would like to know that those in far corners of the world were thinking of them. Also, Bessie shared the same birthday as the Queen Mother—August 4, as she mentioned on her card.

She never expected a reply. The Royal Family would be far too busy to write to a stranger in Canada. But she was wrong. Soon after, came greetings to her from the Queen Mother!

That isn't all. Every year since, the Queen Mother has sent birthday greetings to Bessie on August 4, and Bessie has sent hers to the Queen Mother. Indeed, perhaps the Queen Mother has come to look for Bessie's card almost as eagerly as Bessie. For, though their lives have been very different, there is much that links them—both are widows, both are no longer young, and both find their greatest joy in their grandchildren.

A lovely story, isn't it—and one so typical of a gracious and beloved lady.

THE FRIENDSHIP BOOK

FRIDAY—MARCH 30.

ONE winter's night I found myself hopelessly lost in the fog and in a part of the city I didn't know.

I heard footsteps approaching me, and as I peered towards them, I saw a figure striding confidently through the fog. "Excuse me," I ventured, "but can you direct me?" "Certainly," said the stranger. "I'll do better than that—I'll take you."

Together, we set off through the swirling fog to the address I had given, my guide's hand on my elbow. In less than no time, we were there. "You must know your way about well," I said, thanking him. "Fairly well," he said, and as I turned to face him and held out my hand to shake his, I realised he could not see my hand, or indeed the way we had come. For the stranger who had led me so surely through the fog was blind.

As I heard his footsteps marching away into the gloom, I knew that was why there had been no hesitation. To one who must live in a world of darkness, the way ahead is as clear in the thickest fog as in the brightest sunshine.

SATURDAY—MARCH 31.

THE death of a dearly-loved relative or friend is always heartbreaking, even if your faith in God's goodness remains strong. After all, the separation means the loss of so much that was precious while it lasted.

I pass on a thought given by a friend in the hope that it may bring at least a little comfort:

They are not lost, our well-beloved,
    Nor have they travelled far—
Just stepped inside God's loveliest room,
    And left the door ajar.

APRIL

Sunday—April 1.

ONE thing have I desired of the Lord, that I shall seek after; that I may dwell in the house of the Lord all the days of my life.

Monday—April 2.

IT was to be a very special holiday for Robert and Georgina McLeod. They had first visited Jersey soon after they were married and planned to re-visit all the places they had seen then.

But it was never to be. Only two days after they arrived, Mr McLeod died at 56. I can only imagine how his wife must have felt, far from home and all the familiar, comforting things that are so reassuring at such a time.

A few days later a simple service was held in a Jersey crematorium. In some ways it was the moment Mrs McLeod dreaded most. It seemed like the final moment of parting, and it was all the worse because she knew that when she stepped into the chapel, there would be no one there to mourn her husband.

She was wrong. In the pews sat five women and a man, all strangers to her. It seems they were on holiday, too, and had been in the hotel when Mr McLeod collapsed. They knew how empty the crematorium would be, so they decided that they would go to the funeral. Mrs McLeod never learned their names, and she couldn't thank them properly just then—but oh, what a difference it made to have the comfort of their presence there.

THE FRIENDSHIP BOOK

Tuesday—April 3.

I CANNOT explain why good friends and neighbours fall out. But I do know that, in the nature of things, forgiving and forgetting require boundless grace — and most of us don't have enough.

I recall the story about two sisters who lived in the same town without speaking to each other for over twenty years. When Alice was turned seventy, her sister, Mary, found her own conscience pricking. And when she heard Alice was ill she felt compelled to visit her. From her sick bed, Alice looked sternly at her visitor. At last she said faintly, "Mary, the doctor said I'm going to die. If I do, I want you to know you're forgiven— but mind, if he's wrong, things stay as they are."

Laugh if you like—but before you do, ask yourself if any of your own bridges are in need of repair.

Wednesday—April 4.

I WON'T tell you Mrs Atkins' age, but it's what you might call ripe. Still, she's a game old soul and lives on her own and "manages" for herself.

Her married daughter, Betty, drops in to see her as often as she can. After Betty's done any jobs that need doing, they have a cup of tea together. Betty always has some bits of news for her mother, but really Mrs Atkins isn't terribly interested.

Like many old ladies she loves to talk about her young days and the things that happened years ago.

Betty's heard it all before, oh, hundreds of times. She knows the stories backwards. But she sits and listens, and smiles and nods as if she were hearing the old tales for the very first time.

Bless her patience!

THE FRIENDSHIP BOOK

Thursday—April 5.

I SCAN the headlines, and I think,
"What are we coming to?"
There's so much wrong, it worries me—
Maybe it worries you?
But I must not forget to add
There's such a lot that isn't bad!

Friday—April 6.

THE Lady of the House grins. "Cut yourself shaving again?" she'll ask, or simply shake her head at my clumsiness. But most mornings I have no injuries and for that, I have to thank an American salesman from Wisconsin. A piece of advice his boss had given him seemed to haunt him. It was — invent something people use once, then throw away, and your fortune will be made. But weeks of hard thinking had failed to produce the brainwave.

Then one day as he stood before his shaving mirror, laboriously honing his open cut-throat razor, the idea came to him. Why not a thin blade of steel, sharp as a razor, that could be fixed in a handle, used once, then thrown away?

His friends jeered. Experts said it couldn't be done. But he knew his idea would make his fortune. At last, after eight years of struggling, his safety-razor blade went on sale in 1903. Only 168 were bought, yet in the following year, nearly $12\frac{1}{2}$ million were sold and his fortune was made.

His name? King C. Gillette. When he died 40 years ago, his name was a household word.

To keep on gamely when the chips are down. Never to give up hope. Always to believe the best is yet to be. That was Gillette's motto, and I've yet to hear a better one.

THE FRIENDSHIP BOOK

SATURDAY—APRIL 7.

ONE cold morning twenty-five years ago, John Grant collapsed in the street.

The doctor looked grave and shook his head. John's wife was in tears. John's sister declared in a penetrating whisper, "He's going!"

And at that moment, John half-opened his eyes and muttered, "Oh, no, he isn't!"

After that he made steady progress, and is alive today, retired and taking life easy, but enjoying every minute, and apt now and then to give his sister an affectionate smile and remark, "Sorry! Still here."

How often we can do what others think can't be done!

SUNDAY—APRIL 8.

TURN Thee unto me, and have mercy upon me; for I am desolate and afflicted.

MONDAY—APRIL 9.

NATURE, they say, is red in tooth and claw. I suppose it is, but . . .

Approach a lapwing's nest and the mother bird will drag along the ground at your feet, feigning a broken wing and risking her own life to lead you away from the nest.

Otters, even when they're fully grown, love to play. They will slide down a slippery bit on a river bank and climb back up from the water over and over again.

The cocks of several kinds of bird will fly to the nest where the hen is hatching eggs and offer her a tasty titbit.

It isn't all red and it isn't all cruel.

THE FRIENDSHIP BOOK

TUESDAY—APRIL 10.

NO matter how the rain comes down,
The sky will clear one day.
Though you have worries by the score,
Sometime they'll pass away.
So grit your teeth if life is tough —
At last the smooth will oust the rough!

WEDNESDAY—APRIL 11.

LET me tell you about Dora, who lived alone with her ginger cat called Mr Smillie.

An odd name for a cat? Perhaps. But some years ago Dora had to go into hospital, and what a lot of kindness she found there, not least from the surgeon. He was never too busy to speak to her, and she told him about her home, her neighbours, even the cat which, until it died, had been her faithful companion.

How she missed that cat, she said with a sad smile. The surgeon listened and nodded, for he understood that while he might give her a measure of health, a lonely heart can be a deeper wound . .

One day he appeared with a box under his arm, and handed it to her. What do you think? Inside was a fluffy orange kitten, to take the place of the cat she'd lost! Why, Dora was quite overcome and when she wondered what to call it, decided there was only one name — "Mr Smillie," after the kindly surgeon who'd given it to her and, from then on, "Mr Smillie" was her constant companion.

Last year, Dora passed away. Her beloved cat has a new home on a farm. And I am sure, if she'd wished any tribute to be paid, it would be to the gifted surgeon for whom loneliness is another disease that can be cured.

THURSDAY—APRIL 12.

IN my reading recently I came across an item which intrigued me a good deal. I found it in a life of Alfred Edward Matthews, who died in 1960. A Yorkshire actor, he played many parts in his time, but did not win fame till he was 78, when suddenly he was "discovered" and became a star overnight in Britain and the U.S.A. He kept on acting in plays and film, even when he turned 80 . . . and when he was over 90 he was still drawing huge crowds. It is said he knew more about the technique of light comedy than any other actor alive.

Somebody once asked him how he managed to keep so active and young at heart. "Easy," was the reply. "At breakfast I look at the obituary notices in *The Times*, and if my name's not there I go straight off to the studio and get on with my job."

Not everyone can live like that—but what a fine way to live, doing something, being somebody, enjoying every useful minute right to the end!

FRIDAY—APRIL 13.

QUEEN VICTORIA'S Diamond Jubilee was celebrated in 1897, and it was in the summer of that year the Editor of *The Times* found on his desk a few verses which he merely glanced at before throwing them in the wastepaper basket.

Later, however, he fished the verses out again. Next day the poem appeared in print—it was Kipling's famous hymn *Recessional*, and ever since then it has been sung round the world:

Lord God of Hosts, be with us yet,
Lest we forget — lest we forget!

Very often second thoughts *are* best.

THE FRIENDSHIP BOOK

SATURDAY—APRIL 14.

I'D like to pass on these lines from Miss Finlay, of Templemore Street, Belfast. She found them in a church magazine, and tells me they should be sung to the grand old marching tune of the hymn "Stand up, stand up for Jesus."

> *Get up, get up for Jesus,*
> *Ye sluggards of the Cross;*
> *A lazy Sunday morning*
> *Means certain harm and loss.*
> *If Christians on a week-day*
> *Can rise at half-past seven,*
> *They surely on the Sabbath*
> *Can rise for half-eleven!*

SUNDAY—APRIL 15.

BUT let all those that put their trust in Thee rejoice : let them ever shout for joy, because Thou defendest them : let them also that love Thy name be joyful in Thee.

MONDAY—APRIL 16.

ONE of the prettiest nurses in a large hospital up North is just wonderful — or so the patients declare. She is skilled. She knows her job. She is gentle and kind and cheery, but (unfortunately as she tells everyone) she has a most peculiar relative, Uncle Joe, who says and does the queerest things. Never a day but what this wicked little nurse tells a patient about Uncle Joe—who is wholly imaginary—and has first one patient in tucks, and then the whole ward !

But then, isn't it the little bit extra that always counts for so much ?

Thanks, Nurse !

THE FRIENDSHIP BOOK

Tuesday—April 17.

If you are feeling better than
  You've felt for many days;
If you have had a bit of luck
  Or just one word of praise;
If things for you are not too bad
  And you can laugh or sing,
Or feel that you are fortunate
  To see another spring . . .
Well, if you meet someone you know,
Don't be afraid to tell 'em so!

Wednesday—April 18.

YOU wouldn't think three little weeds would make much difference in keeping a garden tidy, would you? But you would be wrong.

The derelict patch of ground outside the Brownies' meeting hall was an eyesore and eventually the girls decided to take the matter into their own hands and do something about it.

They needed some help with the heaviest work, of course, but they worked steadily day after day, clearing the ground, preparing the soil until the great day arrived when the planting could begin. In no time at all the plot was a picture, but as any gardener will tell you, that is only the beginning. How would they manage to keep it tidy now, after all their work?

That's where the three-weed system came into action. It was agreed that each Brownie, on her way to the meeting every week, would collect three weeds. Just that—no more!

We should never think that the little we have to offer is not enough to be worthwhile—it could make as much difference as three little weeds.

THE FRIENDSHIP BOOK

Thursday—April 19.

DID you happen to see that television programme in February 1972 in which Maurice Chevalier came to life again, and invited us into his home, sang some of his famous songs, made us smile, and suddenly took us by surprise?

The surprise was a moment when he was serious, telling us that the secret of a happy life was to be found in *honesty* . . . being honest with yourself and others, giving of your best, speaking the truth, trying to live the honest, useful life.

Chevalier was a great and much loved entertainer —and also a profound philosopher, for it is impossible to be happy if we do not give to life at least as much as we get.

Friday—April 20.

I SOMETIMES think that we who are older, and have a notion that we are wiser, are groping in a world we have made dark and bleak, and it takes a small child to bring in some light.

This thought returned only a few days ago when I heard what happened in a class of seven-year-olds. They had been told that Judas Iscariot had betrayed Jesus, and that he was a bad man. Evidently wee Jessie did a bit of thinking on her own about this; and quite a few minutes after the story had moved on, she harked back to Judas. "I'm sorry for Judas," she announced to the surprised teacher. "If he was naughty it is very sad, and people ought to have forgiven him and made him happy again, and then he would have been good."

I suspect there are learned Bible students of mature years who haven't yet got quite as far as Jessie.

THE FRIENDSHIP BOOK

SATURDAY—APRIL 21.

FROM overseas come these words of comfort for couples who are not as young as once they were.
Let me hold your hand as we go downhill.
We've shared our strength, and we share it still.
It wasn't easy to make the climb,
But the way was eased by your hand in mine . . .
We move more slowly, but together still,
Let me hold your hand as we go down downhill.

SUNDAY—APRIL 22.

YE seek Jesus of Nazareth which was crucified: He is risen, He is not here: behold the place where they laid Him.

MONDAY—APRIL 23.

SIR WALFORD DAVIES, musician to the King in the reign of George VI, was once asked to sign a student's autograph book.

Sir Walford said, "I will write the two grandest notes in music with which Handel begins his recitative in "Messiah," "I know That My Redeemer Liveth." And he hummed the two notes, "I know," and, drawing the five lines and the staff notation, he wrote in the two notes.

"I know," he said, "has been my inspiration all my life."

Faith is beyond reason, the response of the whole being to evidence of which we feel sure. Some folk ask for mathematical proofs of the existence of God. They forget that all the deep experiences of life; love, friendship, trust and truth go far beyond that kind of proof.

When we say, "I know," nothing can withstand our assurance, neither life nor death.

A CUSTOMER

*Excuse me, sir! Yes, you down there,
I wonder if you've any spare,
I wouldn't mind some fish for tea,
If you have any scraps for me?*

DAVID HOPE

WINDMILLS

    Long since, the mill was built to last,
    Part of a changeless scene,
    For still the clouds go sailing past
    And still the fields are green.
    Many men have come and gone,
    Cared for the land and passed it on.

                                DAVID HOPE

THE FRIENDSHIP BOOK

Tuesday—April 24.

*IF all your plans have come to grief,
  If hope has vanished quite,
If you have toiled and saved and planned—
  And nothing has gone right.
In spite of hopelessness and pain,
With courage high, begin again!*

Wednesday—April 25.

What is optimism?

I could give you a one-word answer. Instead, listen to the story of a young man named Morris Scott. Morris has an incurable illness which means he must live his life from a wheelchair.

Often he'd sit outside his home and watch aeroplanes high overhead. He longed to visit the places they were going, though it seemed like wishing for the moon. But Morris put on his thinking cap. B.E.A. said there would be no difficulty on the flight. The problem was getting him up the steps and aboard the aircraft. That's when the men of the Naval Air Station at Lossiemouth stepped in. They'd a spare set of parachute harness, and they devised a way of adapting it so Morris could easily be lifted into a plane.

Morris saved hard, and at last came the great day of his first flight. A friend took him to the airport. There he was lifted on to the plane for Orkney and the Shetlands. Then it was back to Inverness and home again. It was so successful, he saved for another flight, then a third flight followed, to London and back.

Now this plucky young man in the wheelchair is saving every penny he can spare for a dream flight by jumbo jet across the Atlantic to New York and back again. How's that for optimism?

THE FRIENDSHIP BOOK

Thursday—April 26.

IT was Mrs Margaret Clark's birthday recently She doesn't mind my telling you that she's now 53, and as she looked at all the cards the postman had brought her way, a thought struck her. It was simply that never before had she stopped to consider all the titles we collect as we pass along life's road.

For every card she received bore her relationship to the sender. One came to her as a sister. Another reached her as an aunt. Yet another was sent to her as a niece. In pride of place were those carrying love and best wishes to her as a wife, a mother and a granny

Oh, I daresay it's a thrill to gain another kind of title—to be made a lord or a lady, or to be known as Sir John or Sir James. But, like Mrs Clark, don't you feel the proudest titles of all—and the most worthwhile — are those we already have, each with its precious bond linking us by the deepest ties of all to a loved one?

Friday—April 27.

A SMALL friend of ours came home from Sunday school after her first visit, to be asked the inevitable question by her parents—"And what happened?"

"Oh," said the tot happily, "I learned that God was on the phone."

"On the phone . . . ?" said her astonished parents. Then it dawned. The little girl had learned that God was on "His Throne."

But how truly she spoke. What truer conception of the communication between heaven and earth could we have than speaking on the phone?

Only we may not always listen in!

THE FRIENDSHIP BOOK

SATURDAY—APRIL 28.

*IT'S good sometimes to think of those
  Whose road is long and rough.
The folk who do their best to cope,
  Yet never have enough.
It's good to think. It's good to do
A bit to help such people through.*

SUNDAY—APRIL 29.

THUS it is written, and thus it behoved Christ to suffer, and to rise from the dead the third day: and that repentance and remission of sins should be preached in His name among all nations.

MONDAY—APRIL 30.

A MISSIONARY once told of how she had started a Bible class for girls in a remote African village. It meant a lot of work and a long walk in the hottest part of the day to get there and back again.

The class started with great enthusiasm, but gradually, one after the other, the girls lost interest until one afternoon she found only one member there.

It was too much for her. All that work and effort seemed wasted. Tired and overcome, she leant her head in her hands and wept.

A pair of dark arms crept round her neck and a girlish voice whispered, "Never mind, Miss. Haven't you been telling us the Lord Jesus Himself would have come for one?"

The greatest courage is surely the courage that hangs on even in the face of seeming defeat. Such courage comes from people who have faith that God is fashioning His victories out of their defeats.

MAY

TUESDAY—MAY 1.

THIS thought, passed to me from William Newton of Darlington, is worth pondering, especially by those of us who may grumble about the infirmities that come with passing years, and long for the health and strength that was ours in years gone by.

Says William: The doctor maybe can't make you young again—but he can help you to keep on growing old!

WEDNESDAY—MAY 2.

I HAVE been enjoying a very interesting and very heart-warming little book by Ronald Thomson: *Green Corn, a Caithness Anthology*. Among its examples of prose and verse are lines by Jane Thomson to the Longhope lifeboatmen, and I note that at the end is a saying new to me: *For every sailor lost at sea, a star is born.*

Plainly, this is a poetic fancy. All of us realise that when there is loss of life—at sea or on land—some heart comes near to breaking. Bereavement means parting, and those who remain must surely mourn. Their day has become night.

But life is curiously surprising. Unless we deliberately refuse to be comforted, time slowly brings unlooked-for consolation, unexpected balm for our sorrow and the sore it has created, and the brave heart at last realises a mysterious compensation—a pride in the memory of the loved one lost, an awareness of an enriching sorrow which brings its own deep, inexplicable joy.

And thus in our dark and lonely sky *a star is born*.

THE FRIENDSHIP BOOK

THURSDAY—MAY 3.

WHEN I was a boy, my world was one of few cars and no jet aeroplanes. Even the gramophone was a novelty. What intrigues me is the way small children absorb today's world with such confident ease.

I think this was brought home most vividly the other day when two little girls, one three and the other four, were having a tea party. Said Jean, "My Mum has gone to hospital for a baby. How did she know when it would be ready for her?"

Because of her great age and experience, Miss Moira was slightly impatient with Jean. "Heavens!" she exclaimed. "That's easy enough. The baby just phones when it feels like coming!"

Now, when I was a boy . . .

FRIDAY—MAY 4.

THIS story is about a young man who offered himself for the ministry but was unable to pass the simplest test. He was advised to study hard, and he promised to do so, but he made no progress in a year, and when questioned he said in self defence: "I study about an hour each evening, but I pray for two or even three or four hours that God will make me a great preacher."

It's a sad story, isn't it? I rather think that young man meant well and had noble desires— but the fact is, he was workshy, and had the mistaken notion that one can get where one wants to be by wishful thinking.

And some of us who say prayers even in these days—days when religion is being criticised— make a big mistake, and do no service to whatever church we belong by thinking that we can expect to receive through prayer what comes only after hard work.

THE FRIENDSHIP BOOK

SATURDAY—MAY 5.

I LIKE these lines by Grace Haines:
It's just the jolly, joking things,
The " Never-mind-the-trouble " things,
The " Laugh-with-me . . . it's-funny " things
  That make the world seem bright.
So here's to all the little things,
The done-and-then-forgotten things,
Those " Oh-it's-simply-nothing " things,
  That make life worth the fight!

SUNDAY—MAY 6.

THE Lord is my light and my salvation; whom shall I fear?

MONDAY—MAY 7.

THERE were many congratulations for Rita Rae when she passed her exams at University, but the one which surprised her most came on a card signed " The Three Signalmen."

You see, Rita's home is on the main railway line from Glasgow to Edinburgh, with a signal-box nearby. It's manned 24 hours a day by three signalmen who work in shifts, and from the box they can see the window of the room in which Rita studies.

Often, late at night, they would look across and see her sitting at her books, for hours on end. Many a time it would be well into the small hours when at last the light in her window went out.

So the three signalmen wondered how her exams had gone—and when they heard the results of her studying, they were so delighted they sent her a card with their best wishes.

Heart-warming, isn't it?

THE FRIENDSHIP BOOK

Tuesday—May 8.

MR R. RAWLINSON, of Stockport, now 70, still recalls the old scroll that hung on the wall of his mother's cottage. In many ways it was the secret of that happy home.

The house is small, but human hearts are there,
And for today at least, beneath your care.
Someone is sad? Then speak a word of cheer.
Someone is lonely? Make him welcome here.
Someone has failed? Protect him from despair.
Someone is poor? There's something you can spare.
Your own heart's sorrow mention but in prayer,
And carry sunshine with you everywhere.

Wednesday—May 9.

JOHN NEWTON was born almost 250 years ago. He became a sailor at 11, was flogged for desertion, mocked religion and scorned believers, and was master of his own slave-trader before he was 30.

But the suffering and misery of the slaves tormented his conscience. On the long, slow voyages from Africa, he began to read the Bible. And, at 40, Newton gave up the sea and became minister of a country church. Every week he wrote a hymn for his flock, among them some of the greatest songs of praise we know . . . " Glorious Things Of Thee Are Spoken," " How Sweet The Name of Jesus Sounds," yes, and " Amazing Grace," the hit that thousands of young folk have been singing.

Later he went to a great church in London. There, until he died at 83, the burly old sea-dog with the forthright sermons and kindly heart drew thousands to hear him. How glad he would have been had he known that his message still reaches out so unforgettably.

THE FRIENDSHIP BOOK

Thursday—May 10.

THE Lady of the House was out shopping when Mrs Bellhouse dropped in. She wanted to explain that her husband had a bad cold; so would we mind if she cancelled our invitation to tea on Saturday? Now I had not the faintest inkling that we had received such an invitation (leaving all such matters to the better half), but I passed things off as well as I could.

Not long afterwards the Lady of the House returned, loaded with the shopping and I told her what had happened. "Francis," she said, "there has been some mistake! We were never asked out for Saturday by Mr and Mrs Bellhouse. She must be thinking of somebody else. The awful thing is that if we don't tell them, then the other people, whoever they may be, will turn up on Saturday."

So after a bit of soul-searching, we went to our friends and confessed.

"Good heavens!" exclaimed Mrs Bellhouse. "I remember now. It was the Christies we asked. We meant to have you good people later on."

Well, we all had a good laugh about it—and three couples are still firm friends!

Friday—May 11.

HOME from her first visit to Sunday school, Jean looked remarkably happy. Her mother, rather curious, inquired how Sunday school compared with weekday school, where Jean was in the infants' department.

"Oh," was the eager reply, "I like it heaps better. We haven't to do any sums and you needn't stand in a straight line if you don't want to, and when you leave you don't go to a comprehensive school, you just go to Heaven instead!"

INNOCENCE

Could we but keep our childhood heart,
Innocent and pure;
Could we but love with childhood's love,
Uncritical and sure;
Could we but watch with wonder the sun's new rise,
And see the world around us through our child's clear eyes.

DAVID HOPE

A NEW DAY'S DAWNING

*Dawn is the hour of poetry
That heralds in the day,
When all is wrapt in mystery
Before the sun holds sway.*

*When mists like vapours of a dream
Conceal the commonplace,
Unblemished beauty reigns supreme
In Nature's morning face.*

DAVID HOPE

ISLAND FORTRESS

Along the length of England's coast
The fields slope to the shore;
Only this Cornish bay can boast
A view with so much more—
Perched on its island, soaring high,
A fairy castle against the sky.

DAVID HOPE

THE FRIENDSHIP BOOK

SATURDAY—MAY 12.

IT is over 23 years since I first came upon a few lines written by Dale Carnegie. They are:

"You can make more friends in two months by becoming interested in other people than you can make in two years by trying to get other people interested in you."

I have remembered these lines all this time because I have all along been testing the truth of Dale Carnegie's statement; and now I can back up the truth of his words.

Try it—and see for yourself.

SUNDAY—MAY 13.

AND Jesus said unto them, I am the bread of life: he that cometh to me shall never hunger; and he that believeth on me shall never thirst.

MONDAY—MAY 14.

GRACIE FIELDS, the Lancashire lass who charmed millions in good times and bad, underwent an operation well over 30 years ago, and she wrote at that time:

"You lie in bed saying nowt about nowt while a collection of redhot needles are sticking into you. Folk send flowers, but sometimes you think the next lot will be lilies. Then the surgeons get busy again, and one day you wake up feeling better—things are more rosy and not so lilyish. You begin to sit up and take notice; and suddenly you realise you're getting better and better, and you come to think that it's almost worth being ill because of the pleasure it gives you when you feel you don't need no lilies!"

THE FRIENDSHIP BOOK

TUESDAY—MAY 15.

WE all have secret, cherished hopes—
  We want a sky that's blue,
And think perhaps some far-off day
  Our dreams will all come true.
Perhaps yours will. How nice to find
  Tomorrow is YOUR day!
But maybe things will not work out
  In just your sort of way.
Too bad! And yet a gallant smile
  Can make your living well worthwhile.

WEDNESDAY—MAY 16.

YEARS ago, the Lady of the House and I spent a week of every summer on a lonely farm.

There we relaxed, walked among the hills or sat talking with the farmer and his wife and two big sons—and David, the shepherd.

What a friendly man David was, elderly even in those days, the ideal shepherd, slow of speech yet wise and kindly.

Well, David—who had loved and lost as a young man—died at 70, poor maybe, but highly respected. He was buried on the windy side of the kirk, and there was no headstone bearing his name.

Yet he had an epitaph, one that no storms have erased, carved on many a heart. Though there is still no stone to mark his last resting place, a host of folk still keep his name fresh and green. For he would repair anything for anybody, and even now, in homes far off and among the grandchildren of those who knew him, if anything gets cracked or broken, folk say with an odd smile, "David'll mend it." These four words are a humble man's rare memorial.

What use to David would a worn headstone be?

THE FRIENDSHIP BOOK

THURSDAY—MAY 17.

IT was a great day in Crosslaw Eventide Home, Lanark, when Bob Paterson, the oldest resident, was 100. There was a marquee on the lawn and a cake with 100 candles. There were gifts for Bob, congratulations from the Queen, even a red carnation for his buttonhole. For all of which, needless to say, Bob was mightily grateful and thrilled.

But one thing would have made his day complete —and it was, simply, the sound of bagpipes. All his life, Bob has felt there is nothing quite like the pipes for thrilling a man's heart and setting his feet tapping. Now, at 100 and in an eventide home which he'd never be able to leave, he wondered if he'd ever hear their skirl again.

That's when it happened. Faintly at first, but growing louder every second, came the sound of pipers on the march. Bob just couldn't believe it when through the gates wheeled the massed pipe bands, in full uniform, specially to play for him! It seems the World Pipe Band Championships were being held near Lanark that same week-end. When some of the pipers heard about old Bob, they decided his wish would be granted. And so the finest pipe bands in the world marched off to give an old man the surprise of his life, and if there weren't quite 100 pipers, well, I'm sure there's never been a braver blaw!

FRIDAY—MAY 18.

WHENEVER things go right for me,
I'm lucky — and I know it.
I have a singing heart a while,
I'm happy, and I show it!
If you some sunny days should hit,
Please scatter happiness a bit!

THE FRIENDSHIP BOOK

SATURDAY—MAY 19.

DID I ever tell you the story of Chopin's instantaneous success when, at the age of nine, he played before lords and ladies and in the presence of the Grand Duke Constantine?

"The Wonder of Warsaw," as he was styled, was to play the piano as the last item in a remarkable concert. He wore a fine velvet suit with a lace collar, and looked no more than six when he walked confidently across the stage, seated himself at the piano, played a few chords, found that he liked the tone, and then fascinated and astonished his great audience by his unbelievable skill.

His turn brought tumultuous applause. Little Frederick bowed, smiled, and hurried off the stage. "Mummy, Mummy," he cried excitedly, "the people clapped like anything *when they saw my new collar*."

SUNDAY—MAY 20.

THE steps of a good man are ordered by the Lord: and He delighteth in his way.

MONDAY—MAY 21.

ONE of the legends of our Lord concerns a crippled beggar who went to look at Jesus, but because of the crowds he couldn't even see the strange physician who healed so many. Miserably and, at first, angrily he limped towards his humble home; but, realising his wife, also a cripple, would be sorry he had not seen the Lord, he determined to tell her nothing of his disappointment, and when he went indoors he kissed her.

Instantly, says the old story, she and he became well and strong. Need I point the moral?

THE FRIENDSHIP BOOK

Tuesday—May 22.

*YOU know, as well as I, there are
Some things you shouldn't do,
And yet you keep on doing them . . .
Now isn't this quite true?
No need to preach. I'll simply say:
" Start doing what is right today!"*

Wednesday—May 23.

DR WILLIAM ANDERSON went to Dunbar 50 years ago riding a push-bike, with all his belongings in a case strapped to the carrier. In the years that followed, he won a unique place for himself in the hearts of all who knew him. For all his life his guiding principle was: I must leave this world a better place.

How well he lived up to his motto. When he saw a pensioner struggling home up a brae, he'd stop and give her a lift. And before she got out of the car, he'd press a packet of tea or sugar into her hand, for he always carried a few with him. He arranged for countless parcels of groceries and meat to reach widows and old folk, always anonymously. He gave away TV sets. He even gave up half his lunch hour every Friday for years to go and read to an old blind lady down the road.

But the story I like best about him is of a visit he once paid to an old woman who lay dying in her cottage. He could do little for her, but before he left, he read her Bible to her . . . " In my Father's house are many resting-places . . ." A friend who was with him was struck by the fact he did not say "many mansions." "No," said Dr Anderson afterwards with a smile, " for Jeannie's lived all her life in a but and ben—she'd never be happy in a mansion."

THE FRIENDSHIP BOOK

Thursday—May 24.

Sir Francis Bacon left us this thought over 300 years ago, but it's still as true today:
"It is not what men eat but what they digest that makes them strong; not what we gain but what we save that makes us rich; not what we read but what we remember that makes us learned; not what we preach but what we practise that makes us Christians."

Friday—May 25.

The highbrows are contemptuous. Most of the literary critics of this century ignore her completely, yet some lines from Ella Wheeler Wilcox, the American poet who was born in 1855, will live for many years to come. Like these for instance:

Laugh and the world laughs with you;
Weep, and you weep alone;
For the sad old earth must borrow its mirth,
But has troubles enough of its own.

Saturday—May 26.

Some of us enjoy radiant health and some of us find going about our daily business or doing the household chores anything but easy—we are so soon tired, and what others do quickly requires from us great effort. There are others who are ill in home or hospital, and smiling along is very hard for them.

Here, for all such, is a little 17th century prayer which may help:

Lord, teach me the art of patience while I am well, and give me the use of it when I am sick.

In that day either lighten my burden or strengthen my back.

THE FRIENDSHIP BOOK

Sunday—May 27.

NO man can serve two masters: for either he will hate the one and love the other; or else he will hold to the one and despise the other. Ye cannot serve God and mammon.

Monday—May 28.

TRAVELLING on a train, I once found a paperback lying on the seat. It was "The Real Enemy," written by a French patriot called Pierre d'Harcourt, a Resistance hero who was betrayed while helping British soldiers to escape from France and was sent to Buchenwald, the Nazis' terrible death camp. I will not go into the details of the horrors of the camp or the suffering of the prisoners, but on the last page of the book Pierre sums up all that has gone before by telling the story of the fire in his bunkhouse:

"In the grip of winter, it was tempting to huddle close to the brazier, all they had for heat. But it was fatal to do so. The contrast between the cold outside where roll call could take two hours and the warmth of the fire inside was too much for the prisoners to stand. In time, it led to death Everyone knew it. They knew that to survive they must keep away from the fire. Yet many decided that death was better than cold."

And who lived? Only those, says Pierre, with some kind of faith. He saw it in Christians and Communists. He saw it in people with no religion or political creed, yet who still had some inner core which gave them the will to believe in life when the rest had given up. Indeed, it showed him that though a man may be faced with many great enemies down through the years, the real enemy is within.

THE FRIENDSHIP BOOK

TUESDAY—MAY 29.

WHEN Miss Jane (who is still the sunny side of 80) was off colour for quite a time in the early spring, her neighbour across the road very kindly did her garden. "You're very kind," murmured Miss Jane. "You'll get your reward in due course."

And her neighbour did. Not an illuminated address of thanks or five pounds in notes . . . in fact, nothing—apart from the colourful show which summer brought, and which would not have been visible from the gardener's windows had he not done his good deed in the spring!

WEDNESDAY—MAY 30.

YOU can't keep on.
You've tried in vain.
You cannot cope —
You've failed again.
Yet some quiet voice is whispering still,
" I'll try once more — I will, I will!"

THURSDAY—MAY 31.

THE gift that meant most to Grannie was a new Bible from six-year-old Kenneth.

Kenneth had chosen it himself, and he wanted to write a message inside the front cover. He knew that was the done thing. His father had recently been given a book by a friend and there on the fly-leaf he found what he was looking for. Though he wasn't at all sure what it meant, he copied it carefully into Grannie's Bible, showing it to no one.

Well, Grannie was a bit surprised to read: " With the compliments and best wishes of the Author "—but she's quite sure the message is true, for all that!

ONCE IN A LIFETIME

We walk on ice from coast to coast
Above the lake's dark waters;
A fearful thrill, but how we'll boast
To unborn sons and daughters!

DAVID HOPE

TO CATCH A TROUT

*With wary trout to lure from the stream
And banks where a boy can lie and dream,
The hours of a long, long summer day
Slip all too rapidly away,
But leave in memory's golden store
A radiant glow forever more.*

DAVID HOPE

JUNE

FRIDAY—JUNE 1.

THESE lines were sent by a friend on the other side of the Atlantic.

How true they are and how badly they need to be taken to heart today.

A gossipy tongue is a dangerous thing
  If its owner is thoughtless at heart;
She can give when she chooses full many a sting
  That will painfully linger and smart.
But each gossipy tongue would be baulked in its plan
  For causing distress, hurt and tears
If it weren't helped out by the misguided one
  Who possesses two gossipy ears.

SATURDAY—JUNE 2.

I HEARD the other day there are people who dial TIM not because they want to know the time but simply to listen to a voice. Sometimes they even say a warm, " Thank you," to the recording.

Sad, isn't it, and a timely reminder that there are no end of men and women who long for the sound of a friendly voice. Much is done to help people who cannot afford any comforts, who are short of food, or, in winter, of fuel, and the State looks after many of their physical needs.

But, rich or poor, loneliness eats into the heart and breaks the spirit, and there is far more of it than some of us realise. If we know anyone living alone, especially somebody who rarely or never gets out of doors, it costs us so little to look in now and then. We can make them feel we care, and what a difference that makes!

THE FRIENDSHIP BOOK

SUNDAY—JUNE 3.

HAVE mercy upon me, O Lord; for I am weak.

MONDAY—JUNE 4.

HERE'S a story with a smile.

It comes from the Rev. Alexander Caseby, of Anstruther, and it's about a minister who announced to his congregation that his sermon was to be on the subject of "Truth."

"Now," said he, "before I begin, has everyone read the 35th chapter of Matthew?"

Half of those present raised their hands.

"Good," smiled the minister. "You're just the folk I want to speak to. There's no such chapter!"

TUESDAY—JUNE 5.

A NEIGHBOUR of mine spends much of his time in his garden, which is a picture.

He's a quiet, thoughtful man, and the other evening we chatted a while over the wall.

"It's a strange thing," he said, "but when I see a fine cabbage I've grown, or a good row of carrots or strawberries, I feel proud. Yet when I look at a single rose, I feel humble."

I wonder why. Could it be that, on the one hand, when he remembers the care with which he planted seeds, watered the young plants, and tended the growing vegetables the results fill him with a sense of his own achievement? And on the other hand, when looking at a rose, is he aware of a living miracle, a thing of delicate beauty, in the creation of which he played such a small part?

I cannot say. But when I mentioned it to the Lady of the House, she understood. I think every true gardener will.

THE FRIENDSHIP BOOK

WEDNESDAY—JUNE 6.

IT'S never ALWAYS fine, you know—
The sun goes in or out.
Life's kind to you, then most unkind,
You know it, without doubt.
This simply means enjoy the best,
And try to smile through all the rest.

THURSDAY—JUNE 7.

SOME time ago a friend in Edinburgh sent me some poems by a man called Walter Murray.

Walter describes himself as semi-retired, enjoying life and writing poetry now and again because it gives him pleasure. A cheery picture, isn't it, of a man with little to worry about?

Well, I enjoyed the poems so much I was determined to find out more about Walter. I learned he'd been a steel erector. One day he was working high on the massive chimney stack of Portobello Power Station.

There was an accident. Next thing, Walter was spinning through space. He plummeted over 200 feet. Nobody knows how he survived smashing into the ground. All his ribs were broken and a foot was completely crushed. After he got out of hospital, life was a struggle, and he had five youngsters to bring up.

Then, ten years ago, paralysis set in and Walter went to live in the Thistle Foundation in Edinburgh. I'm told he is a basket-maker of some skill now. And he says he's a lucky man to have so many fine friends in the home and outside.

Really, there are two Walter Murrays. The one I'd been told about and the one I found out about for myself. Quite a difference in them, isn't there? And a lesson!

THE FRIENDSHIP BOOK

FRIDAY—JUNE 8.

IT was a perfect day for an outing.

There was only one snag. One man kept grumbling—the coach went too quickly or too slowly. His meat at lunch was tough and there wasn't enough of it. His tea was too sweet. The grumbler was a man standing six foot two in his socks. In the first few hours he caused irritation to all the other folk who were out to enjoy every minute.

Then a little old lady changed everything.

When the giant muttered something about the driver, she called out, "Don't take any notice of him! He'll grow out of it when he's bigger!"

From then on the big but little-minded man never expressed a complaint!

SATURDAY—JUNE 9.

HAVE I ever mentioned MacAndrew?

He drives a tipper lorry. One day he rattled along with ten tons of gravel, swung into a building site, backed over a temporary road of old railway sleepers—and went an inch or so too far. The rear wheels sank into the mud and the front wheels rose high in the air.

MacAndrew climbed out of his cab. Other workmen gathered round, grinning. "Now what are you going to do, mate?" asked one.

MacAndrew stroked his double chin, thoughtfully. "Oh," he said at last, smiling, "this is a bit of luck. With you chaps to help, we'll have her on the level in no time . . . but while she's still in the air I'll grease her underneath. Haven't had such a good chance for a while."

MacAndrew is not only a truck driver but a philosopher. For he makes the best of the worst, and sees an opportunity in every difficulty.

THE FRIENDSHIP BOOK

Sunday—June 10.

I WILL lay me down in peace, and sleep, for Thou, Lord, only makest me dwell in safety.

Monday—June 11.

I'D like to give you her name.

But I'll just say she lives in Lanark, and is the mother of two growing boys.

Recently, an old tenement was being demolished in the town. It was the place where she'd been born and brought up. When she heard it was coming down she thought again of her early days there, of her mother and father, of the friends who lived up the same stair—and of her home's one brass tap at the sink in the window.

How she hated it! For, almost from the time she could walk, it was her job to keep the tap bright and clean. And no sooner had she got it shining than it was all splashed again. But her mother never allowed her to shirk her task.

As time passed, she realised it was her mother's way of teaching her that, irksome though it might seem, her duty must be done. And last week she went to have one last look at her old home. The place was derelict. Then, in the broken window, above a sink full of rubble, she saw the old brass tap, tarnished and brown.

It brought everything back to her. And though it may not be the done thing for a respectable married woman (which is why I can't name her!), she unscrewed the tap with her nail file and carried it triumphantly home.

Now it rests on her sideboard, screwed to a block of wood. Need I say it shines proudly as ever, just as its message has done down through the years.

THE FRIENDSHIP BOOK

TUESDAY—JUNE 12.

THE nanny-goat was wandering free near the pretty white cottage. She did not appear to be tethered in any way. Then we noticed that a tiny white kid was tethered to a tree nearby.

It gave its mother a call from time to time, and every now and then she went back to examine the kid and to see that all was well.

There was absolutely no need for the nanny-goat to be tied. For between mother and child God has made certain ties which are stronger than rope or even steel.

WEDNESDAY—JUNE 13.

SAY a cheery word to somebody you meet
 Lend a hand to someone living in the street.
You will find that always, always it is true,
What you give to others comes right back to you!

THURSDAY—JUNE 14.

THIS smile comes from our old friend Mrs Christie, who lives in Westgate, Bucksburn, and is known to all as Auntie Annie. She's a widow who lives alone, and sometimes she doesn't keep too well. But we know few who meet life more cheerfully.

Auntie Annie was across at her neighbour's the other day. While she was there the children came in from school.

"Have you heard the story about the butter?" asked young Louis. Auntie Annie confessed she hadn't. "Well," he replied, "I won't tell you in case you spread it!"

I'm glad I'm not the only one to be confronted by conundrums from the youngsters next door.

THE FRIENDSHIP BOOK

FRIDAY—JUNE 15.

SHAME'S a powerful weapon!

I'm thinking of a schoolgirl who went to a concert by a famous musician and at the stage door asked the violinist for his autograph. "Sorry, not now," he replied impatiently. "My hands are tired." Instead of taking offence, the schoolgirl replied, "My hands are tired, too—with clapping!"

She got the autograph, and the two parted good friends!

SATURDAY—JUNE 16.

YEARS ago a young lad was sent by train to collect his office payroll. He'd persuaded the engine-driver to let him travel in the cab—and now, near the end of the trip, the money was no longer under his coat. It would certainly mean the sack.

Near to tears, he begged the driver to reverse along the railway. All the way back, Andrew scanned the verge of the line. Then, as they crossed a bridge, he saw the money lying on the bank of a rushing stream.

That boy was Andrew Carnegie. He went on to become one of the richest men in history, worth 300 million dollars. Yet it was years before he could bring himself to talk about that terrible day he lost the wages. And all his life he wondered—what might have been if the packet had fallen in the water and been carried away.

So he vowed he would try never to be too hard on a young man who made a mistake, and never to judge anyone too harshly. What's more, every time he passed over the bridge where he lost the payroll he renewed his vow.

If Andrew Carnegie couldn't afford to judge too quickly, can you?

THE FRIENDSHIP BOOK

Sunday—June 17.

GIVE thanks unto the Lord; for He is good: for His mercy endureth forever.

Monday—June 18.

HAVE you heard this story of Clara Barton, founder of the American Red Cross?

One day a friend reminded her of a particularly mean trick that had been played on her. Clara looked puzzled, and her friend was amazed.

"Surely you remember that, Clara!" she declared.

With a thoughtful frown Clara said firmly, "No, I distinctly remember forgetting that!"

Tuesday—June 19.

HAVE you ever thought how big our planet is?

Over 55 million square miles of land. Over 140 million square miles of sea. Population at least 3500 million. Figures too large, perhaps, to have any real meaning. Oceans, mountains, deserts, rivers, crowded cities . . . what a world!

But when Michael Collins, an astronaut in a recent moon probe, was 200,000 miles out in space, he peered from a window in the command module and had no end of trouble trying to find our planet! When he did find it, it was shining like a tiny, precious jewel in the black void, small enough to be lost among millions of other worlds.

It makes you think, doesn't it? Makes you wonder if, after all, there's enough room down here for all the bickering and argument and shouting. Makes you wish we could learn to get along together, all of us, and enjoy the priceless heritage which is ours.

THE FRIENDSHIP BOOK

WEDNESDAY—JUNE 20.

> *WHEN climbing up the mountains*
> *Or bathing in the sea;*
> *When hiking, fishing, lazing,*
> *Wherever you may be,*
> *May summer skies be o'er you,*
> *May there be lots of fun;*
> *And, please, still keep on smiling*
> *When holidays are done!*

THURSDAY—JUNE 21.

IF you know Cowcaddens, in Glasgow, you're sure to know Dallas's restaurant.

Every week, hundreds of people have lunch there, and it was there, some time ago, a few teenagers sat chattering at their table.

An elderly woman approached and asked if she might sit down at the empty place beside them, for it was the only one left. She sat quietly until the waitress brought her soup.

And there, amid the bustle of the restaurant and the chatter of the youngsters, the old woman folded her hands and bowed her head to say grace. The teenagers looked at her then, one by one, they lowered their heads, too and joined her in silence.

Were they humbled at the old woman's example? Or did it stir the memory of when they, too, never failed to say thanks?

I cannot say. But I am told that every day the same old lady comes into Dallas's for lunch. She's in her 80's, a retired school teacher. And no matter how crowded the restaurant, she never fails to bow her head before she eats and give thanks for the meal before her.

No one will be the worse for sharing *her* table!

THE FRIENDSHIP BOOK

FRIDAY—JUNE 22.

ONE day recently, wee Jean, aged four, was late home.

She had been visiting her Aunt Mary, only two doors away, so her mum wasn't worried, but she did say, " I was wondering where you were, dear."

" Oh," said Jean in the matter-of-fact way children have. " I heard Auntie Mary say Elspeth had died, so I went along to comfort her mummy."

Jean's mum was taken aback. She knew Elspeth, only three, had died in hospital, but had been careful not to mention it. " Darling," she murmured, " whatever could *you* do to comfort Elspeth's mummy?"

" Oh," said Jean, " I just climbed on her knee, and she hugged me and we cried together."

SATURDAY—JUNE 23.

A LITTLE thought is often worth a lot of effort. This old but true saying came to mind when I saw this verse framed on the office wall of a successful businessman I was visiting. I asked him if I might copy it. Here it is, with his compliments :

There's many an industrious man
  Who never gets ahead,
Because he does not think or plan,
  But trusts to luck instead.
He's not a slacker nor a shirk,
  This plodder in life's grind,
But though he always minds his work,
  He never works his mind.

SUNDAY—JUNE 24.

O LORD, our Lord, how excellent is Thy name in all the earth!

THE FRIENDSHIP BOOK

Monday—June 25.

MR CURRIE blesses the day he didn't run over a potato in Barrhead!

A Scottish minister, he happened to be driving along behind a lorry loaded with potatoes. As it rounded a corner, one fell on to the road.

Most of us wouldn't have given it a second thought. But Mr Currie stopped and picked it up, one of the finest Kerr's Pinks he'd ever seen. So he took it home and planted it in the manse garden. That was eight years ago.

When he lifted his crop he'd 27 fine potatoes. He kept them all and planted them the following spring. This time his crop was more than 200 Kerr's Pinks. So he took them to the family farm on the Isle of Arran, and to this day every Kerr's Pink grown on the farm is descended from the lost potato on the road. What's more, they are the best potatoes Mr Currie has ever tasted.

Mr Currie must have often preached a sermon on the parable of the lost sheep. In its way, this is the parable of the lost potato, and I'm sure there's a fine message in it, too.

Tuesday—June 26.

WHEN things perplex you, and the way ahead is darkened by doubt and fear, try to remember Christopher Columbus.

When he set out on his famous voyage of discovery, he didn't know *where he was going*.

When he arrived on the strange shores of America, he didn't know *where he was*.

When he got back, he didn't even know *where he'd been*.

And yet he knew beyond a shadow of doubt that he had found a great, new world.

THE FRIENDSHIP BOOK

WEDNESDAY—JUNE 27.

DAN STEWART, a friend of mine in the U.S.A., sends me this thought for all pilgrims on the road of life. He tells me the writer is unknown, but for all that there is no mistaking the message:

When someone walks beside us
On the road that we must keep,
Our burdens seem less heavy—
The hills are not so steep.
The weary miles pass swiftly
As bravely on we stride;
And all the world seems brighter,
With someone at our side.

THURSDAY—JUNE 28.

I HEARD the other day of a lad of 17 who refused to take his shoes to mend unless his mother wrapped them in brown paper—not in part of a newspaper. He said he wasn't going to be seen carrying his shoes to be repaired. How important or high society he thought he was, I cannot imagine; and why he should imagine it to be disgraceful to do the small task asked of him is quite beyond me.

I am reminded of a story they tell of Abraham Lincoln. When he was President of the United States an ambassador called on him and was astonished to find the first man in America cleaning his shoes. "But, sir," exclaimed the shocked ambassador, "surely the President does not clean his own shoes?"

The whimsical Abe grinned and replied with a witty query, "But, Mr Ambassador, if the President does not clean his own shoes, whose shoes should he clean?"

False pride gets nobody anywhere.

THE FRIENDSHIP BOOK

Friday—June 29.

BING CROSBY tells a witty story of how he was once playing golf when he and a friend—a Roman Catholic priest—were caught in the rain. It was no ordinary shower, and at last Bing said, " Father, this is just too bad. Can't you pray for fine weather?"

With a wry smile—and a twinkle in his eye—the priest replied, " Sorry. That is not my department—that's management. I'm in sales."

In the oddest way, as you will realise at once, there is profound wisdom here as well as wit. The business of the whole world is in God's hands. Our job is to hand to others the love of God, advertising it and giving it publicity, not only by what we say, but by what we do and the way we live.

Saturday—June 30.

WITH innocent assurance a little girl walked into the palatial hall of a world-known company and asked to see the managing director. An amused secretary had a word with that great and hidden personality, and eventually the child was shown into his office. There she explained that her class at school was raising money for homeless children and would he please contribute.

The busy man, tickled pink by the sheer audacity of his visitor, put a pound note and a 5p piece on his desk. " Take which you like," he said.

Without hesitation the little girl picked up the coin, saying, " Mummy's told me always to take the smaller of two gifts." Then, with a ravishing smile, she added, " And so's I don't lose it, I'll wrap it up in this bit of paper."

It made the big man's day!

JULY

Sunday—July 1.

THE Lord will give strength unto His people; the Lord will bless His people with peace.

Monday—July 2.

DAILY, thousands of pensioners bless the ladies of the W.R.V.S. who bring them meals on wheels.

Others in the W.R.V.S. use their cars to take the old and sick to clinics and hospitals, or to visit relatives. Needy families are given a holiday.

Yet all of this might never have been but for the vision of one remarkable woman, Lady Reading, founder of the W.V.S. I will never forget a story she told me about a young woman who joined the W.V.S. in London during the war, and who was terrified of air raids.

One night, safe in an air-raid shelter, she heard the sirens. She tried to forget her fears as she gave out blankets and soup to families from nearby tenements. Then word came an old woman had refused to leave her home on the top floor. The young woman volunteered to go and sit with her.

Less than an hour later the tenement was destroyed by a bomb. Lady Reading told me that when they found the young helper's body, her fingers were still gripping the handle of a teacup. The girl who was terrified of air raids had been sitting with that old lady, comforting her with a cup of tea as German bombers devastated the city.

Two years ago Lady Reading herself died. I'm sure she would have wished for no other memorial than that the ladies in green should carry on with their mission, no matter where it leads.

THE FRIENDSHIP BOOK

TUESDAY—JULY 3.

NOT long ago I received a letter from South Africa. It was beautifully written by an elderly lady who wanted to tell me about her daughter's trip to Britain. There were ten pages of neat, small handwriting, and my wife read them all aloud to me. Then, having finished, she looked up and said, "I wish there were some more pages!"

I had to smile because in those few words my wife had summed up the whole art of letter-writing. Some people bore their friends with their letter—concentrating far too much on what little troubles they themselves have rather than picking out the pleasant things that have occurred to them or their friends and neighbours.

It is the letters that are human documents which fascinate, and it is the small yet charming things and events that make the best reading. According to Charles Dickens, Sam Weller summed up letter-writing in one sentence when he said: "She'll vish there vos more, and that's the great art o' letter-writing." It is, indeed.

WEDNESDAY—JULY 4.

YOU never know when one you know
Will finish life's short run.
If you intend to cheer a friend,
It's time to get it done!
A kindly deed, a word to say?
The time is now. Do not delay!

THURSDAY—JULY 5.

A THOUGHT for today — and every day. A smile is a curve that can set a lot of things straight!

THE FRIENDSHIP BOOK

Friday—July 6.

WHAT is conscience?

I've heard many a definition from pulpit and platform. I have read even more in books written by the greatest philosophers who ever lived.

But one of the most memorable, if perhaps the most light-hearted, comes from a schoolboy to whom that question was put not so long ago.

"Conscience," he said solemnly after a moment's thought, "is something that makes you tell your mother before your sister does."

Saturday—July 7.

IF you love your child you will make him do as he is told.

Allowing a child do what he likes when he likes and how he likes is not kindness—it is laziness or indifference on the part of the parent; and in the end the child grows up selfish and boorish, and the parents suffer because of his bad behaviour.

All this seems obvious and elementary — but there are tens of thousands of parents who won't take the trouble to teach a child to obey, and to obey promptly and with a good grace.

I was reading only the other week that a noted child specialist had been saying: In any critical illness, the child who has been taught to obey has a four times better chance of recovery than the undisciplined child.

It's worth thinking about.

Sunday—July 8.

FOR thou shalt eat the labour of thine hands: happy shalt thou be, and it shall be well with thee.

DAYS IN THE PARK

>Here, in the past there must have been
>Many a time a festive scene,
>With folk in silks and laces;
>And happiness is still the same,
>Although today we cannot claim
>To have the airs and graces.

>DAVID HOPE

FIRST DAYS

*Slender, graceful and shy,
Poised and ready to fly,
Soon you'll be strong and proud,
Swift as a silver cloud.
Freely you'll offer then
Friendship and help to men.*

DAVID HOPE

THE FRIENDSHIP BOOK

MONDAY—JULY 9.

CAN you imagine it?

Try to think what life would be like day by day for you and me if, say, there was a tax of 25p an hour on sunshine; if the law limited us to having no more than twenty flowers in our garden; if water had to be bought by the gallon; if we had to book supplies of fresh air in advance; if only dukes, earls and bishops were permitted to walk—and the rest of us were compelled to drive cars; if a backdoor chat with a neighbour cost 10p for the first two dozen words and 1p per word thereafter.

Is it all too silly to contemplate?

Perhaps so—but does it not serve to remind us that some of the best things in life cost nothing, not because they are worthless, but because they are priceless?

TUESDAY—JULY 10.

BEFORE me, in the window of a junk shop, was a large earthenware bowl, brownish outside, yellow inside.

It took me back down the years to my great-aunt Maggie's kitchen where, on Fridays, she made and baked bread. I was very little when, seeing a huge bowl before the kitchen fire, I asked questions, and was told that having kneaded the dough, Auntie Maggie had left it there to rise. "You can't see it and you can't hear it, and you can't hurry it," she told me. "But give it time!"

How vividly that scene sprang before my eyes as I looked at the old bowl in the junk shop and how clearly I recalled the philosophy of an old woman, long dead, who knew one of life's greatest secrets—have patience.

WEDNESDAY—JULY 11.

I THINK I'll put the world to rights—
It's in a dreadful mess.
I'll shout. I'll lead — I'll show you folks
A thing of two, I guess . . .
But some delay there'll have to be
Till I've put right what's wrong with me!

THURSDAY—JULY 12.

THERE'S many a happy way of saying thank you. But one of the most moving I have heard about came from the congregation of Carrick Knowe Church, Edinburgh.

After 33 years, their minister, the Rev. Donald Chalmers, was retiring. On the Sunday he preached his last sermon the church was packed. Typically, his sermon was based on love, for if ever a man loved his flock, Mr Chalmers did. Now he was about to leave them, for his health hadn't been good recently.

Slowly he raised his hand and, for the last time, gave the benediction. Then, on impulse, the organist began to play. As one, the choir and congregation rose and began to sing . . .

The Lord bless thee and keep thee;
The Lord make His face to shine upon thee
And be gracious unto thee;
The Lord lift up His countenance upon thee
And give thee peace.

All Mr Chalmers could do was stand in the pulpit, head bowed. And if it had not been for the tears that misted his eyes, he would have seen that many of those before him were weeping, too.

I have never before heard of a congregation pronouncing a benediction on their minister— yet could they have found a lovelier farewell?

THE FRIENDSHIP BOOK

Friday—July 13.

NOT long ago, a friend of mine visited Denmark on holiday.

Late one night he left his hotel in Copenhagen for a breath of fresh air. As he strode through the darkness, he saw a figure crouched in the shadows of a shop door.

Perhaps the man was ill and needing help, he thought. But when he drew closer, he found to his surprise that the man was kneeling there in prayer. In English, my friend apologised for disturbing him. But the stranger explained that more than 25 years before, his only son, a student, had worked with the resistance. One night the German forces retaliated. His son had been shot down in this very doorway.

So every year since, on the anniversary of that day, the man came to the shadowed shop door late at night, when all was quiet and still. There, for a few minutes, he knelt to remember his boy.

This year, he was making his pilgrimage for the 28th time, and I know my friend felt moved and proud to have shared something of it with him, and now with us.

Saturday—July 14.

ST PETER was puzzled one day.

There seemed somehow to be an error, and he had always kept the books accurately. In the end he took his problem to God, saying: "I don't like having to mention this, but according to a census there are more people in Heaven than I have let in—unless my books are wrong."

God smiled. "Don't worry, Peter," he said. "I gave you the keys of the front door—but I keep the key to the back door myself!"

THE FRIENDSHIP BOOK

Sunday—July 15.

GIVE unto the Lord the glory due to His name; worship the Lord in the beauty of holiness.

Monday—July 16.

A COUPLE I know had a ding-dong argument while visiting Newby Hall in Yorkshire.

My friend, who knows a bit about wood, was examining a finely carved door. "It's a grand bit of chestnut," he exclaimed admiringly.

"Oak," his wife corrected.

"Chestnut!" my friend said warmly.

So they began arguing till the lady who was showing the party round the Hall intervened smilingly, saying, "Yes, it is an interesting door—chestnut on one side, oak on the other."

There are at least two sides to every question!

Tuesday—July 17.

NOT long ago, a girl was driving a tractor to help her brother with his work in a field. Suddenly, something went wrong. The tractor tipped over and the girl was trapped underneath it. Her brother grasped the tractor and raised it just enough for his sister to scramble clear.

That's all there is to it, except this. When the young man went back to the field later that day and tried to show exactly what had happened, he just couldn't lift the tractor one inch!

I'm not going to preach about this. But I do think it is a dramatic proof that we can all do more than we think we can if we really have to.

If it comes to the push, and if you have courage or patience or determination enough, you can do the thing that needs to be done!

THE FRIENDSHIP BOOK

WEDNESDAY—JULY 18.

THE two of you were long in love—
How sweet those precious years.
Now one has gone and one is left—
How hot your bitter tears!
What if the happy years you knew
Had only been a very few?

THURSDAY—JULY 19.

I'M sure Grannie Gibb, of Castlemilk, Glasgow, has never visited Carlogie Hotel, near Carnoustie.

Indeed, I doubt if she's ever been inside a hotel in her life. She lost her husband while still a young mother, and had to work hard to bring up her three children. Tommy, the eldest, was killed in France in 1944. Helen died on the eve of her wedding. Davie, the youngest, was lost at sea while serving with the Merchant Navy.

So Grannie Gibb is all alone now, and not even one grandchild to gather in her arms. But every day you will find her surrounded by the children from round about, and it is to her that young mothers turn for advice and reassurance. She could have become bitter. Instead, she wore a smile, even though her heart was breaking.

What has all this to do with Carlogie Hotel? Well, when I had tea there recently I couldn't help thinking of Grannie. On the lawn is a sundial and, engraved round the edge, I read these words:

Turn your face towards the sun, and the shadows will fall behind you.

What a difference it would make to so many sad, discouraged people if they followed the sermon on the Carnoustie sundial, and the example of that old Glasgow widow.

THE FRIENDSHIP BOOK

FRIDAY—JULY 20.

TILL recently, I thought I knew the meaning of the phrase " The weakest goes to the wall."

It seemed quite obvious the weakest got pushed back by the strong and suffered in consequence.

But no. It dates back over the centuries to the days when churches had no pews. Everybody had to stand or kneel, except the old and infirm. For them, many churches provided a wooden bench or a stone ledge against the walls, and while the young and strong were expected to stand, the weakest " went to the wall," where they could sit.

Isn't this a reminder that it's the privilege of youth to bear the burden of the old ; and isn't this as it should be? The society where younger people are eager and willing to shoulder responsibility for, and give help to, the old and needy, is a strong, healthy, warm-hearted society which deserves to enjoy life to the full.

SATURDAY—JULY 21.

WHEN life isn't very easy, we can either grumble or make the best of things.

I am thinking of a friend in Canada, not young, and with his fair share of troubles. But his letters are invariably cheery. In one recent letter he told how the folk in his town, Hamilton, had just come through a 63-day bus strike.

When the strike was over, one man told his wife that, just to get his own back he wasn't going to take a bus. " I'm going to walk behind it," he said, " and save thirty-five cents."

" Well," said his wife, " why don't you walk behind a taxi and save a dollar and a half?"

Folk who can make light of annoyances generally come out best in the end!

THE FRIENDSHIP BOOK

SUNDAY—JULY 22.

FOR Thy loving kindness is before mine eyes: and I have walked in Thy truth.

MONDAY—JULY 23.

NOT long ago a friend of mine came across this little verse by J. V. Neither he nor I know who J. V. is, but the message in the lines is worth passing on, anyway.

Somewhere there's someone
  Who dreams of your smile,
And finds in your presence
  That life is worth while.
So, when you are lonely
  Remember it's true:
Someone is thinking . . .
  Thinking of YOU?

TUESDAY—JULY 24.

I HAPPENED one day recently to pick up Phil Drabble's interesting book, "Badgers At My Window," and found this recipe for cheerfulness:

"My cure for personal worry is to pause and think what I worried about exactly a year ago to the day. The fact that it is usually quite difficult to remember, cuts the present trouble down to size."

It's an idea. I am not sure we can always act on it, but it does remind us that in days gone by we had troubles and problems and fears which seemed immense and intimidating and caused us a lot of misery at the time . . . and that somehow we survived them. Indeed, somehow we not merely survived them, we eventually forgot all about them.

Isn't there a thought here for you and me?

THE FRIENDSHIP BOOK

WEDNESDAY—JULY 25.

SOME folk have lots of cash to spend,
  Some folk haven't half enough.
It doesn't seem quite fair to me
  That many find life tough.
But, whether you are short or not,
  Be thankful for the wealth you've got!

THURSDAY—JULY 26.

MANY a thrilling story has come back to us about Man's first visit to the moon.

Yet unaccountably, one which is surely among the most moving and significant of all is known by only a few.

It happened in July 1969, when Apollo II took its crew soaring into space to become the first men ever to set foot on the moon. One of them, Buzz Aldrin, determined that such a great step must be marked in a unique way.

So, in the Apollo spaceship, he carried with him a tiny silver cup, a small flask of wine, and a crumb of bread in a plastic pack. When he took his first steps on the moon, he called back to mission control at Houston, asking for a few moments' silence, and inviting all who were listening to give thanks in whichever way they wished. Then, laying the bread and the silver cup before him, he poured out the wine, watching it curl slowly up the sides of the cup.

That is how the first liquid ever to be poured on the moon, and the first food to be laid there, were the bread and wine of Communion.

It is a lovely story and surely it symbolises, as nothing else could, the faith of the astronauts, and the unseen bond linking them with the millions who waited thousands of miles away.

RIVERSIDE

> Beside a river I'd like to dwell . . .
> To wake to morning melodies,
> Hear timber creaking in the breeze,
> Mark the tide, its ebb and flow;
> In the trees the seasons know . . .
> A riverside house would please me well.
>
> DAVID HOPE

THE FLYING MACHINE

Our sons will need both skill and nerve
To pilot planes like this,
While discipline and will to serve
Will never come amiss.

Such qualities are theirs, as ours,
  But may they also find
The means to use Man's growing powers
  For good of all mankind.

DAVID HOPE

ON PARADE

The men go swinging past, as they have done
  In peace and war, where'er the call has been.
In distant lands beneath an alien sun,
  And now they proudly march to guard the Queen.

DAVID HOPE

THE FRIENDSHIP BOOK

FRIDAY—JULY 27.

ONE bright morning recently, I met the postman at the door.

Afterwards, I walked down the garden path looking at my wife's flowers, and also watching the postman, who delivered mail at No. 15 and No. 19, but not at No. 17.

My heart was heavy. We know the little lady at No. 17. She keeps fit in spite of her age and of living alone. But there is an ache in her heart. Her only relatives are her grandson and his wife and three children, living many, many miles away; and the biggest thrill she ever gets is a brief postcard at long intervals.

Every morning she peers through her window. But nowadays there are not more than half a dozen cards a year, and the little lady sighs and tries to smile as if it didn't matter.

But it does!

SATURDAY—JULY 28.

I LIKE the story Professor William Barclay tells about the old lad who'd taken over an allotment which was a wild patch of overgrown weeds, rubble and dear knows what.

He turned it into a pleasant corner of flowers and vegetables, and the minister, happening to see the transformation as he passed one day, said: "What wonderful work God can do, John."

"Yes," said John. "But you should have seen it when he had it to himself!"

SUNDAY—JULY 29.

BE of good courage, and he shall strengthen your heart, all ye that hope in the Lord.

THE FRIENDSHIP BOOK

Monday—July 30.

Do you recall all the fuss about the Census?

My friend, John Bunney, of Consett, tells this story, about the Census man who, calling at a house inquired, "How many are there living here?"

Wiping her hands on her apron, the woman who opened the door began to count. "Well, now," she said. "There's my husband and me. There's Susan and Jim. There's Auntie Brenda and——" There she was interrupted by the caller "I'm not interested in names. It's numbers I want."

"Sorry," said the housewife. "There are no numbers in this house—only people."

Tuesday—July 31.

I'D like to tell you about Mrs Boyle's father.

In his day he was a famous man. His name was Hugo Innocenti. He was at the top of his profession, and spoke seven languages fluently. Yet he was not a businessman or professor.

You may well have seen him, for he travelled the world as Darti — a circus clown!

Though he made millions laugh, his own life was tragic. His marriage was a failure. He was plagued with depression. In the end, he was badly injured during a performance in the circus ring, and was doomed to spend his last years in a wheelchair, living in poverty, with only his pet dog, Lucky, for company.

He died recently, at 84. And as this man who made millions laugh was laid to rest there was only one mourner.

To all who saw him, Hugo's life was filled with laughter and fun and fame. But the truth, as Mrs Boyle told me sadly, was so very different.

Things aren't always what they seem . . .

AUGUST

WEDNESDAY—AUGUST 1.

*HOWEVER long the journey,
    However rough the way;
However dark the midnight,
    There'll come a break of day.
Keep on with trust, smile as you go,
Dawn may come sooner than you know.*

THURSDAY—AUGUST 2.

I HAVE never met Jim's mother.

But I am able to tell you she had four children. Two of them died young. Her only daughter now lives in Australia, and keeps urging her mother to join her and her husband. Jim's mother longs to go—longs to see her daughter and her three grandchildren, but she refuses. Her excuse is she must go to see Jim now and then.

And Jim? Jim is in prison, and will be there a long time. He is a wastrel. He was cruel to his wife, and she left him. He committed serious crimes, and caused his mother untold sorrow and shame and suffering. Yet she cannot think of forsaking him. Other mothers will understand the reason—*she loves him*.

I confess I am not tremendously interested in Jim, but I *am* interested in a mother whose love knows no bounds. Such a love is too deep and noble to say much about—one just realises dimly that a mother's love is in its way a miracle.

One other thing I can tell you about Jim's mother. It is that she once said to me in a letter, "You can never love anybody too long or too much."

F

THE FRIENDSHIP BOOK

FRIDAY—AUGUST 3.

HOW can you tell if you're growing old?

A friend of mine was observing recently how times have changed since he was a boy, not only with the coming of jet aircraft and television, but instant potatoes and frozen food, too.

"Man, Francis," he said with a smile, "I remember when a pie was set on the window-sill to cool, not to thaw!"

Yes, times *have* changed!

SATURDAY—AUGUST 4.

DID I ever tell you the story of the Aberdeen landlady?

A new student had just arrived to lodge with her. She showed him to his room—clean, neat, but furnished with only a bed, chair and table. No pictures on the wall. No ornaments. Not even a carpet on the floor—just bare boards, scrubbed until they were white.

The landlady must have seen the hesitant look on the student's face. But she simply smiled. "Laddie," she said, "that's your room. And if there's anything else you need, just come to me and I'll show you how to do without it!"

Well, that young student went on to become Professor Baillie, one of the best-known names in Scottish learning.

But he vows the lesson he learned from his Aberdeen landlady was one of the most important of his life.

SUNDAY—AUGUST 5.

THE meek will He guide in judgment; and the meek will He teach His way.

THE FRIENDSHIP BOOK

Monday—August 6.

I DON'T know even the name of the youngster who destroyed my complacency, a boy of five or six who tagged himself on to me as I walked to the office the other morning. " Going to work?" he asked, as if he had known me all his short life.

I said I was.

" What d'you do?"

" Oh, I sit at a desk and write."

"*That* isn't working," he retorted scornfully. " You should see my dad—he *works*. He sprays roads with tar, and gets all messy—and it's really hard work, but he gets a lot of money. They shouldn't have to pay *you* much. My dad's really useful. How could we manage without roads?"

Luckily for me, he turned off to school down a side road . . . and I went humbly on my way.

Tuesday—August 7.

EVERYONE feels sorry for hospital patients, especially if they're not getting on as quickly as they had hoped.

But I am often sorry for their visitors, too. Sometimes there are few things in life harder than saying good-bye when visiting time is up.

Of course, a visit to somebody you love can be a pleasure, and if the patient is making good progress you may both feel full of hope and thankfulness.

But if the patient isn't as well today as yesterday, if there's pain or weakness which brings tears, if you just can't think what you can safely say without making your loved one apprehensive, or if you can see them going downhill, what agony it is to say good-bye.

You've to be brave to be a patient. But it can take a different kind of courage to be a visitor.

THE FRIENDSHIP BOOK

WEDNESDAY—AUGUST 8.

THE Lady of the House and I agree this old rhyme is as true today as ever:
Folk talk about a woman's sphere
But there's no place in earth or heaven,
There's not a task to mankind given,
There's not a blessing or a woe,
There's not a whispered yes or no,
There's not a life or death or birth
That has a feather's-weight of worth
Without a woman in it!

THURSDAY—AUGUST 9.

JOE and Jean occasionally got a visitor. Not regularly, of course, but when he did decide to drop in, they always made the old ginger tom-cat perfectly welcome.

He bore all the marks of long years of battle, with a damaged tail, half his right ear missing and scars across his face. Joe and Jean nicknamed him Scruffy. Now and again Scruffy would look in, partake of the meal he was offered, lounge for a little by their fire and allow himself to be petted before going on his way.

One afternoon when they were entertaining old Mrs Watson, who lived much farther along the street, Scruffy happened to drop in too. "Oh, that's my pussy!" exclaimed Mrs Watson. "That's my *Fluffy*, although sometimes I don't see him for days at a time."

So *Scruffy* he was to his adopted friends, but *Fluffy* he remained to his real owner. Sometimes the eye of love is blind; so blind that it can no longer see reality. And maybe it is a good thing that it should be so. Beauty is in the eye of the beholder.

THE FRIENDSHIP BOOK

FRIDAY—AUGUST 10.

I WAS listening the other day to a good lady who was busy criticising a certain minister. Now I don't know the minister she was talking about, so maybe all that she said against him was true. The only thing I could say for sure is that she herself has not been inside a church for years. So it seemed to me she had a double standard: one for herself, and perhaps the same standard for the world of commerce; but never lifting a finger to help, she still expected a totally different standard and a far higher standard from the Church. I left her, thinking to myself how godly the ungodly expect others to be!

SATURDAY—AUGUST 11.

RONNIE was the boy friend who seemed most likely to run off with Mavis. Very recently she informed her mother that he had everything—good looks, academic honours, a safe job with fine prospects, money in the family, and the wit which tells him just what people like to be told. " So why not marry him?" asked Mum.

Mavis, I understand, shook her head and smiled sadly. " No," she said. " I think life's already too comfortable for him. Things have been too easy all the way along. He's already a bit smug and self-satisfied—gosh, what'll he be like at forty? On the whole "—and here Mavis was *very* serious (which is rare for her)—" I'd like to marry someone who still has his way to make, and I'd like to help him."

Well, Mavis may have something there. Many a marriage is that bit stronger and more meaningful for that little bit of hardship that had to be overcome together.

THE FRIENDSHIP BOOK

Sunday—August 12.

IF thy brother trespass against thee, rebuke him; and if he repent, forgive him. And if he trespass against thee seven times in a day, and seven times in a day turn again to thee, saying, I repent; thou shalt forgive him.

Monday—August 13.

THE idea just popped into my head, and though tempted to go on looking at the evening paper, I jumped up there and then—and did it in less than no time.

What I did was not quite world-shattering. I merely wrote half a dozen lines to my old friend Arthur, telling him that only that very afternoon I'd been talking with a man who had asked after him. That man had recalled the two years when he was taught by Arthur—long years ago now; and he recalled the way in which Arthur stood up for the things he believed in. " He shaped me for good," said the man I met that afternoon; and it seemed to me that I ought to tell Arthur what that old schoolboy of his had said.

So I wrote that letter, and the Lady of the House and I strolled round to the pillar-box and posted it.

How glad I am I did what I did. It cost me only a stamp, but it reached Arthur when he was in hospital—quite unknown to me—two days after he had had an operation and was feeling very sorry for himself!

That letter worked wonders. It warmed Arthur's heart and set him thinking his way back into the past. He's feeling perky again now. I repeat, how glad I am I did what I did when I felt I ought to do it!

DECISIONS

> The names are queer but the country's great
> (Capel Curig! Portmadoc!),
> Symbols on the map translate
> To tumbling stream and towering rock.
> Time to take a well-earned rest,
> And choose the route that seems the best.
>
> DAVID HOPE

ADVENTURES

> One little brood, a world complete,
> Seeing the world on their own flat feet.
> Till mother thought, " I'm not so fond
> Of the concrete. No, I like the pond.
> It's fine to see the Queen and travel,
> But grubs are scarce among the gravel.
> It's back to the mud for you and me,
> And tails up all to catch our tea."
>
> DAVID HOPE

THE FRIENDSHIP BOOK

TUESDAY—AUGUST 14.

AFTER their honeymoon a young couple moved into their new home—a little old terrace house which for weeks before their wedding day the happy pair had brushed and scrubbed and polished till it shone like new. Over forty years later the street was condemned, and the day came when that man and wife had to move out.

Although they knew their home was to be pulled down, they cleaned it from top to bottom. Then, with tears in their eyes, walked proudly out of that spotless house only days before it was a heap of rubble.

Why did they do it? I'm not going to answer my own question. I leave it to you.

But if everyone had a spirit like theirs, what a different place this land of ours would be.

WEDNESDAY—AUGUST 15.

I CALLED to see a business acquaintance a few days ago.

The matter we discussed made it necessary for him to consult his pocket diary. We agreed on a date towards the end of this year, and as he was noting it on a blank page, I could not help seeing on the next page some words which intrigued me so much that eventually I pointed to them.

My friend smiled. "So easy to forget," he said. "Much too easy. It keeps me thankful and sympathetic—reminds me to do a bit extra when and where I can. You'll know what I mean. I had my op. five years ago, and every first of the month since I've written these words in my diary. Silly? Well, possibly. But I keep it up."

The words, repeated a dozen times a year, are: *I was in hospital once. I must remember.*

THE FRIENDSHIP BOOK

Thursday—August 16.

*I OFTEN think how nice to be
An extra special V.I.P.
But wealth and fame have passed me by—
I'm not quite certain how or why.
Should greatness come at last, maybe
I'd much prefer being simply me.*

Friday—August 17.

Do you say lucky white heather's sheer superstition?

Mr Lionel Pywell doesn't! And it all started with his sore back. Apparently Lionel, who drove a grocery van around Callander, in Perthshire, for years, suddenly fell victim to rheumatism. Everyone confided secret remedies which never failed—but nothing would shift his pain.

Then he thought to himself, maybe it's lack of exercise. So, being a man who does nothing by halves, he decided to climb Ben Ledi! My goodness, it was a struggle. But manfully he toiled.

And just as he neared the top, out of the corner of his eye, what do you think? On a wee hillock he saw a clump of pure white heather!

He gently eased a root from the earth, took it back down the mountain to Callander and planted it at the door of the church. It's blooming there bravely today.

And the odd thing is that, whether it was the thrill of the find that made him forget his pain, the exercise or, of course, the luck of the heather itself, Lionel realised as he straightened up after planting it that his sore back had gone—and, moreover, he hasn't had a twinge since.

So next time you've backache, simply climb a mountain, find white heather—and who knows!

THE FRIENDSHIP BOOK

SATURDAY—AUGUST 18.

I CAME across a few words the other day which struck me as remarkable—remarkable in themselves and because the writer is Svetlana Alliluyeva, Stalin's daughter. This is what she has to say:

"I was brought up in a family where there was never any talk about God. When I was grown up, however, I discovered it was impossible to exist without God in one's heart. I came to that conclusion myself, and without anybody's help or preaching. As a result, a great change came over me, and I ceased to have any regard for the chief dogmas of Communism."

SUNDAY—AUGUST 19.

IN everything give thanks: for this is the will of God in Christ Jesus concerning you.

MONDAY—AUGUST 20.

AT Linburn, near Edinburgh, you will find the workshops and training centre for the war blinded.

One of the men who live and work there began making a repair to a piece of furniture the other night while his wife was out. Darkness had fallen by the time she returned, to find her blind husband still busy. "Goodness," she exclaimed impulsively, "you're working in the dark. Why didn't you switch the light on?"

No sooner had she spoken than she realised what she had said. But her husband only smiled. "Mary," he replied softly, "there's no need to switch on the light. It's always light for me."

Not, you will notice, "it's always dark."

THE FRIENDSHIP BOOK

TUESDAY—AUGUST 21.

OUR old grandfather clock had been stopped for only a day when my wife said, "You know, I never heard that clock ticking till it stopped."

It made me think. It also made me wonder how many of us take things and people for granted till we lose them. Does any man, for instance, know how dear his wife is, how much he depends on her.

Does a mother realise how much the clutter and the noise of a young family mean to her until they have spread their wings? Does a teenager know what the old familiar faces and places mean to him until alone and friendless, he sets foot in a strange town?

Once our old clock is going again, I fancy we'll never again take its friendly tick for granted.

WEDNESDAY—AUGUST 22.

LORD, tell me what I ought to do,
    And give me strength to see it through.
Lord, when some chore I'd like to miss,
    Show me how worth while it is.

THURSDAY—AUGUST 23.

ONE motto often found on sundials is simply:
    The time is later than you think.

And it's true. In youth we feel we have ages before us. In mid-life we hope we shall live a long time. In age we pretend we are fit and well, and that the heart will go on beating almost for ever.

But the truth is that, for one reason or another, our end may be very close at hand, however young or old we are. Therefore—and this is the point—if we intend mending our ways, if there is anything which needs to be done or said, it is high time the thing *was* done or said . . . before it's too late.

THE FRIENDSHIP BOOK

FRIDAY—AUGUST 24.

IT was a happy group of people picnicking on on the beach. When they went on their way, they were careful to carry off all the pieces of paper and cellophane. But, I noticed, they left some scraps of food and it was interesting to sit quietly and to notice the order of precedence after the picnickers had gone.

First came a dog, who did not look a bit hungry; but he picked up one or two tasty morsels and left the crusts alone. Next came the gulls, and when they had gone I thought nothing could possibly be left, but I was wrong. Last of all came the little birds, which had been watching from a safe distance. I sat there until the last and littlest visitor was satisfied. And I thought about this marvellous world and how every creature has its place.

SATURDAY—AUGUST 25.

JEAN MacNALLY, of Belfast, sends me a story about a tombstone inscription in Northern Ireland.

Remember, Man, as you pass by,
As you are now, so once was I,
As I am now, so you shall be,
Prepare for death and follow me.

Not very cheery. But, for a while at least, Jean tells me, visitors to the churchyard read it with a smile. For someone had added two more lines with a piece of chalk:

To follow you I'd be content,
If I only knew which way you went!

SUNDAY—AUGUST 26.

SUFFER the little children to come unto me.

THE FRIENDSHIP BOOK

Monday—August 27.

THIS thought was voiced long ago by a Frenchman, but I have never forgotten it.

He said, " When a friend laughs it is up to him to tell me what makes him happy. When he weeps it is up to *me* to find out what grieves him."

Good advice, isn't it?

Tuesday—August 28.

I HAVE visited St Vincent's eventide home in the little Highland town of Kingussie only once.

It stands on a hillside overlooking the River Spey, in a sunny spot among the trees. There's always a friendly welcome from the cheerful nuns who care for the old people there.

If you are lucky, as you pause inside the door you might hear a ringing tenor voice singing a fine old song, " Bonnie Strathyre," perhaps, or " Westering Home," or " When You Come To The End Of A Perfect Day." Even as you listen you realise that whoever he is he can be no ordinary singer, but one richly gifted. As you peep through the door you will see, to your surprise, he's the parish priest!

He is, in fact, the great Scottish singer, Canon Sydney MacEwan. As you know, the records of his voice have made him famous, and loved, the world over. But, long before he went to Kingussie a few years ago, he announced there were to be no more records. Now the voice that thrilled millions is bringing quiet joy to the old and sick, and leading the praises in a little church in Badenoch.

Though far from the limelight now, who can doubt that, as he serves his Highland flock, his life has never been happier?

THE FRIENDSHIP BOOK

WEDNESDAY—AUGUST 29.

NOW, this is wrong and that is wrong
Life's really very sad.
This awful world, the folk you meet,
Can quickly drive you mad.
So why not try with all your might
To find a few things that are right?

THURSDAY—AUGUST 30.

I DON'T think many of you will know the secret of Sandy MacDougall's magnet.

Sandy often writes to me from his home in Wilmington, U.S.A. His letters are always cheery. Yet for as long as I've known him he's been a prisoner in his wheelchair, a victim of an illness which has paralysed almost his whole body. Indeed, he types his letters with difficulty by using one finger on his left hand.

That's where Sandy's magnet comes in. Before his wife, Dot, goes off to work, she leaves a sandwich beside him and a can of lemonade in an ice bucket beside his chair. Of course, Sandy can't bend to lift up the can. So when it's time for his snack he lowers his magnet on a string till it snaps home on the can. Then he just pulls it up!

Sandy gets such a kick out of his magic magnet that he insists on demonstrating it to all who call, and is highly tickled at his own ingenuity!

There are many ways of looking at misfortune. Who can doubt Sandy's is the brightest?

FRIDAY—AUGUST 31.

HERE'S a thought from Wendell Phillips, the American multi-millionaire. In life, as in a mirror, you never get out more than you put in.

SEPTEMBER

SATURDAY—SEPTEMBER 1.

TOM FLYNN worked in the plastic surgery unit at Bangour Hospital, in Scotland.

Many patients brought there were terribly burned, and Tom saw the pain they suffered when they were lifted to have their burns dressed. It had to be done, of course. But oh, how Tom wished there could be an easier way.

Then one day he was sitting at tea in his home when his mother stepped across to the window and pulled down the blind. That's all. But it gave Tom an idea—why not devise a table, working on the same principle as a roller blind so bandages could be rolled under and then round the patient without the need for lifting?

That night, Tom began putting his thought into action and, though there were many setbacks, the day came when the first table was being used in the new burns unit in Bangour Hospital. You can judge what a boon it will be from the fact that already inquiries about it have come from hospitals all over the world. But Tom won't earn a penny from it, for he has decided to enter the priesthood.

All this would have made Tom's mother so proud. Alas, two years ago both she and his father died. Yet in a way Tom's table is her memorial. For if he hadn't happened to see her pull down the blind that night, the thought that will bring blessing to thousands might never have been.

SUNDAY—SEPTEMBER 2.

CREATE in me a new heart, O God; and renew a right spirit within me.

THE FRIENDSHIP BOOK

Monday—September 3.

LET me tell you about William and Isa Kater.

Recently they celebrated their golden wedding. Friends, relatives and neighbours were there, of course. But so many other people from the district dropped in to shake hands and wish them well, there were more than 300 people in the hall.

Strangely, though, there were no gifts for the old couple. Why? Well, William and Isa had passed on a special message—no presents, please. Instead, anyone planning a gift was asked to consider donating to the church building fund. The news got round and it seemed the whole neighbourhood wanted to add to the kitty.

Nobody was more surprised than William and Isa when it was revealed the church fund was no less than £1125 richer from their happy thought. A golden wedding indeed.

I wonder if you feel as humble as I do when I ask myself if my friends would think as much of me as so many people obviously think of William and Isa.

Tuesday—September 4.

SUPPOSE each of us was born with a little gadget growing on our shoulder and from the moment of our birth it counted off the number of minutes left to us, beginning, say, with two million and going down to one million, five hundred thousand, a hundred thousand, ten thousand, fifty, twenty, ten, five, four, three, two, one, zero!

A bit unnerving, isn't it?

But the thought occurs to me that as the minutes were counted off and the number left to us steadily decreased, you and I would use each minute to the utmost, wouldn't we?

THE FRIENDSHIP BOOK

WEDNESDAY—SEPTEMBER 5.

TO have a job, and hold it down;
To have a loving wife;
To have a friend your griefs to share
Is much in this brief life.
To have a hobby, and a bit
Of faith in times of stress,
This, for a man like me, is wealth,
This is, indeed, success.

THURSDAY—SEPTEMBER 6.

WHAT'S wrong with Walter as a name?
I ask, because Walter Watson, though his birth certificate calls him that, is never Walter to his wife and friends. They all call him Arthur. Not because he doesn't like the name of Walter. But because he can neither hear nor speak, and must lip-read every word others say to him.

Now, it seems that Walter is one of the most difficult names of all to lip-read successfully. It can be confused with all sorts of other words, such as water, weather, winter, and so on. So a change had to be made and, after much trial and error, Walter found about the easiest name to recognise was Arthur! So Walter became Arthur, and Arthur he has been ever since.

Try it for yourself. Simply stand before a mirror, and say both names aloud. When you "see" the name Walter, you'll understand what I mean. And when you "see" Arthur in the mirror, all will be clear.

Can you imagine what it must be like never to hear even your own name? In a way, the simple story of why Walter became Arthur has given me a new and deeper insight into the problems of those who must live in a silent world.

THE FRIENDSHIP BOOK

FRIDAY—SEPTEMBER 7.

I WONDER how many people would attend church these days if John McBirnie were preaching. He died in 1616, and has been described as "a godly, zealous and *painful* preacher."

Painful? Because he spoke the truth, and saw his duty as not to entertain, but to stir the mind and heart. I cannot help wondering if part of our trouble today is not due to our fear of stern discipline and of seeing ourselves as we are.

SATURDAY—SEPTEMBER 8.

MR W. McCULLOCH, of Prestwick, tells me the story of Joseph Scriven, the Irish odd-job man who was nicknamed, "The man who saws wood."

Apparently Joseph's saw was never still. Cutting up logs for a neighbour's fire. Mending an old body's gate. Making wooden toys for the poor children in his neighbourhood.

Yet, though a friend to all, Joseph's own life had its share of sadness.

His sweetheart was drowned on their wedding eve: enough to embitter the kindliest of men. But, though his health was not good, Joseph simply went on helping others.

And, from the depths of his sorrow, he fashioned something else, not with his saw, but with his pen—something infinitely more enduring than anything he ever made in wood. It is the hymn we all learn as children—"What A Friend We Have in Jesus . . ."

SUNDAY—SEPTEMBER 9.

REJOICE in the Lord alway: and again I say, Rejoice.

THE FRIENDSHIP BOOK

Monday—September 10.

A SMILE to begin the week with!
A friend of mine heard it from a policeman who declares it happened to him not long ago.

It seems he was standing near the post office one afternoon, when an elderly lady asked him to see her across the busy street.

He smiled reassuringly. "There's a zebra crossing just up the road," he said.

"Oh, well," retorted the pensioner. "I hope he's having better luck than I am!"

Tuesday—September 11.

WHAT does a bunch of pink roses mean to you?
To one woman, they mean more than words can say. A florist was telling me that for years he has delivered a bunch of pink roses every few weeks to a house in a quiet street. There's never any message with them — yet they carry their own.

The woman's husband is skipper on a deep-sea trawler. On his trips far out into the North Sea, to the Atlantic, or the Arctic waters above Iceland, the going is always hard. Often it is dangerous.

Every fisherman knows that, bad as it may be for him, it is worse for those who wait and wonder at home. So this skipper has found a lovely way of assuring his wife all is well. When the holds are full and the nets are drawn in for the last time, he radios back to headquarters, asking them to order a dozen pink roses for his wife. The order is passed to the florist and at once the roses are sent to the skipper's home.

Whenever they arrive, his wife knows her husband is on the homeward journey.

That's the message of the pink roses. I cannot think of a happier one.

THE FRIENDSHIP BOOK

WEDNESDAY—SEPTEMBER 12.

DO a little kindness,
Forget it overnight;
Go about your business,
And find, to your delight,
That somebody, remembering it,
Has warmed your kindly heart a bit!

THURSDAY—SEPTEMBER 13.

ALEX. BARBOUR'S a van salesman and he and his wife, Annie, have three boys, John, Alex. and Ronnie, who emigrated to Canada and are all doing well out there.

But wait. In the small hours of a Friday some time ago, Mr and Mrs Barbour were awakened by someone knocking on the front door. "Goodness," they thought. "Who on earth can that be at this time of night?" So Alex. got up, and what do you think? There on the step, with a smile like a slice of melon, was young Ronnie! Of course, his mum had to get the kettle on, and while she was busy, there was a knock at the back door. She answered it this time and found John, their oldest boy. Yes, and a few minutes later the door opened —and in walked Alex.

All three had come all the way from Canada to see their mum and dad for the week-end! They went to a football match with their father on Saturday afternoon. On Sunday morning they sat in the old family pew in the church, and how proud their mother was as she saw the astonishment and smiles of the congregation.

Then it was off to catch the plane back to Canada again, and who can doubt the Barbour boys left behind them two thrilled and happy parents, and a lot of admiration from all who know them?

THE FRIENDSHIP BOOK

FRIDAY—SEPTEMBER 14.

I'VE heard many a definition of faith.

Some have come from philosophers. Others from wise and experienced ministers. But the most light-hearted came from my neighbour's 11-year-old boy.

He swept up to the kerb on his bike as I arrived home from the office the other evening. "Mr Gay," he asked, "Can you give me an example of real faith?" I was a bit suspicious of the grin he couldn't quite hide, but shook my head.

"Faith," he went on, with a laugh, "is a bald man going into a chemist's shop for a bottle of hair-restorer and asking the chemist to bring him a comb at the same time!"

Then, ducking the cheerful swipe he richly deserved, he was off—leaving me to share the chuckle with the Lady of the House.

SATURDAY—SEPTEMBER 15.

THE important thing in life is not what happens to you—but what you do with what happens.

I heard recently about a man, born blind, who might well have told himself there was no use trying—he could never hope to be much. But he studied hard, went to university and took degrees at Oxford, Harvard and Paris.

Since then he has published several books. He was an important man in his own field when somebody, immensely impressed, exclaimed, "Goodness! All this, and you are blind! What would you have achieved if you could see?" The answer was unexpected. With a smile, the blind man said, "Most probably, nothing at all!"

Every handicap can be a cross or a challenge!

THE FRIENDSHIP BOOK

Sunday—September 16.

SHEW me Thy ways, O Lord; teach me Thy paths.

Monday—September 17.

EVER heard of a sunshine bag?

St Andrew's Church, Turriff, looking for a novel way to raise money for a good cause, gave each family in the church a little bag and asked them if for every day the sun shone, they'd put a penny in it. Then, at the end of summer, the bags were gathered in and the money used to provide sunshine for others.

I'm told Turriff didn't have the best summer on record by any means, yet when the sunshine bags were emptied there was £300 in them, every penny a thank-offering for a sunny day.

Tuesday—September 18.

I RAISE my hat to the average man. He seldom gets praise or criticism but keeps on being respectable, paying his income tax, going to his job five days a week, doing that job conscientiously, gradually owning his home, remaining in love with his wife, doing his best to bring up his children and give them a good start, lending a hand to a neighbour in need. And so on.

All of which some might not think impressive. But it is this friendly, decent, good-natured man with a humdrum job who is, after all, the backbone of the country, the source of our true wealth, the chap on whom politicians and business firms rely for honest thinking and prompt payment. And, in the last analysis, it is he who gets most out of living.

THE FRIENDSHIP BOOK

WEDNESDAY—SEPTEMBER 19.

*IT'S hard to grin when things go wrong.
It's hard to hide a fear.
It's hard to keep on keeping on
When tragedy looms near.
At all such times it's hard to smile,
But always, always it's worthwhile.*

THURSDAY—SEPTEMBER 20.

IT'S said the younger you learn a lesson, the longer it will be remembered.

I feel that pupils of South Queensferry school will, in years to come, realise how true that is. For, day by day, they are learning a lesson in courage from their headmaster, Mr Peter Somerville.

Some time ago Mr Somerville suffered two strokes, which almost cost him his life. He was left paralysed down one side. Doctors warned him he might never walk again. It seemed he would never again be able to take up the work to which he had dedicated his life — giving children a good grounding not only in education, but in character, too.

Yet even as he lay gravely ill, he had made up his mind he would be back in his old place. I cannot tell you how much of a struggle his first steps from bed were—but I do know every little victory in his fight back was, to him, a challenge to do better next time.

Within months the headmaster was back at his desk. True, he had to use a calliper and a stick to help him. But he had more than ever to offer his pupils, for as they saw him going about the school they would realise the problems of life cannot be met by running away, but by facing them with courage.

HARVEST GOLD

*Folk in cities strive for wealth,
But why they do it puzzles me;
Not for peace of mind or health,
Or aught worthwhile that I can see.
The finest gold in my belief
Is sunshine on the ripened sheaf.*

DAVID HOPE

A DOG AND HIS BOY

Learning to trust, learning to play,
Growing a little more every day.
Learning to share—the good days and bad—
There's so much a dog can teach a lad!

DAVID HOPE

THE FRIENDSHIP BOOK

FRIDAY—SEPTEMBER 21.

THE Lady of the House was busy in the kitchen.
In the living-room the television was still switched on, and I found myself watching the boxing match in which Ken Buchanan defended his world title in New York.

Now, I don't know much about boxing, but I could not help admiring the skill of the young Scots lad, yes, and his pluck, too. But it's something altogether different that I really admire him for. As world champion, Ken was invited to all kinds of victory celebrations in New York, to parties with celebrities, and to lavish hospitality of the kind most of us only dream about. Yet he turned all the offers down.

Why? "Because," he said, "I must be home in two days—it's my wee boy's birthday."

As I say, I don't know a lot about boxing—but that simple remark tells me so much about Ken Buchanan.

SATURDAY—SEPTEMBER 22.

HERE'S a tongue-twister with a moral—
I'd rather be a could-be
If I could not be an are.
For a could-be is a maybe
With a chance of touching par.
I'd rather be a has-been
Than a might-have-been, by far,
For a might-have-been has never been
But a has-been was an are!

SUNDAY—SEPTEMBER 23.

O LORD, my God, in Thee do I put my trust: save me from all them that persecute me.

MONDAY—SEPTEMBER 24.

AT the risk of losing all my friends in the ministry, I repeat this tale as it was told to me.

It's about Johnnie, aged eight, who told his mother he wanted to be a minister when he grew up.

"A minister?" his mother gasped. "Why, Johnnie, I'll be so proud, and so will your father. But whatever made you decide on that?"

Johnnie shrugged his shoulders. He seemed a bit taken aback that his mother should make such a fuss. "Well," he explained, "it looks as if I'll have to keep on going to church all my life anyhow—and it's harder to sit still in a pew than to stand in a pulpit and shout!"

TUESDAY—SEPTEMBER 25.

WHAT makes childhood friendships so precious? The kind of friendship, for instance, shared by six lads at Kent Road School, Glasgow, more than 50 years ago. They were inseparable at school and at play, and, though they could not know it then, they were to be inseparable in death, too. For five of the boys laid down their lives with the H.L.I. in the First World War, three of them on the same day—July 12.

And the sixth? He is Bill Crawford, who spends most of his time these days tending his garden in Chryston, Lanarkshire. As the only survivor, he somehow feels his life was only spared through the sacrifice of his friends, and he has never forgotten them. Every year when July 12 comes round, he makes it his personal day of remembrance, and in a Glasgow paper you can read the tribute Bill pays annually to the fallen five.

Old soldiers never die, they say. Nor, in the heart of Bill Crawford, do old friends.

THE FRIENDSHIP BOOK

WEDNESDAY—SEPTEMBER 26.

WHENEVER life's grimly unkind,
  And my days are as dull as can be,
I wish, how I wish, that the times
  Were somewhat less cruel to me.
But when the harsh grind gets too bad,
I think of the pleasures I've had!

THURSDAY—SEPTEMBER 27.

A PILE of dishes waiting to be washed? Is it a chore you'd happily do without? Before you answer, think of Mrs Christina Hamilton, Douglasdale, East Kilbride.

Mrs Hamilton had four of a family. For her and her husband, it meant setting six places at the table, and six sets of dishes to wash three or four times every day. Though the family all weighed in now and again, it was Mum, of course, who usually had to cope.

Then one by one her family left home and married. At first she'd five places to set. Then four. Then three. And then, when the last of the family left, there were only two places to set.

But here's the strange thing. Often, even when only she and her husband were left at home, Mrs Hamilton would find herself absent-mindedly setting six places at the table again—and when she realised what she had done she would lift the dishes away, sit down in her chair and weep. How empty the house seemed, and how quiet.

Now Mrs Hamilton sets the table only for one, for her husband is dead. At first she couldn't bring herself to set it at all. For somehow the table was the heart of her home, and it was there, above all, she realised she was alone.

I'm sure every wife and mother will understand.

THE FRIENDSHIP BOOK

FRIDAY—SEPTEMBER 28.

THE Lady of the House picked a four-leafed clover the other evening.

"Francis," she said, "why should it be lucky?" I'd to confess I'd no idea. Then, the very next morning, in came a letter with this verse from Miss Margaret Thomson.

The first leaf is for patience,
The second leaf for pluck,
The third for perseverance—
And the fourth leaf is for luck.

Notice only *one* leaf for luck!

SATURDAY—SEPTEMBER 29.

THE other evening I was involved in a lively argument between a friend and his three teenage sons. Father was losing the battle for the elders when I walked into the trap. "While I have every admiration for young people," quoth I, "it does seem to me the problem is getting worse." Without a word the oldest son disappeared, and returned with a large tome. "Listen to this, Mr Gay," he said, and quoted:

"Children now love luxury, they have bad manners, and contempt for authority. They show disrespect for their elders, and love chatter in place of exercise. They no longer rise when their elders enter the room, but contradict their parents, chatter in front of company, gobble up dainties, cross their legs and tyrannise their teachers."

Who said that? Why, Plato, in 400 B.C.!

SUNDAY—SEPTEMBER 30.

I SOUGHT the Lord and He heard me, and delivered me from all my fears.

OCTOBER

Monday—October 1.

ARE you trying your best, but getting nowhere? If so, there is something for you in these lines from Mrs McCulloch, of Dennistoun, Glasgow :—

Who scales the mountain does not always climb—
The winding path slants downward many a time.
Yet each descent is higher than the last—
Has thy path fallen? That will soon be past.
Beyond the hill the road leads up and on—
Think not thy path for ever lost or gone.
Keep striving onwards—if thine aim be right
Thou canst not miss the shining mountain height.
Who would attain to summits still and fair,
Must nerve himself through valleys of despair.

Tuesday—October 2.

DID I ever tell you of a hero who helped shape my life?

He did not win a V.C. in any war. He never rescued anybody from drowning, or climbed Mount Everest or hit the headlines. The only memorable thing he ever did, as far as I know, was to kill himself at the age of 84 by sliding down a banister just to show his great-grandson he could do it!

I know he ought to have had more sense. The fact is my hero of long ago lived—really lived—every moment of his waking hours. He was a small-town solicitor, but he was always doing something besides his job—a quiet, friendly little man whom the young folk adored. And he kept young to the very end, and adventurous, too, and merry of heart in spite of sorrows and troubles.

What a way to live! What a way to die!

THE FRIENDSHIP BOOK

Wednesday—October 3.

DON'T worry—it may never happen.

Familiar words—yet there's a story behind them.

It started when, instead of demolishing a chapel in Cross Street, Manchester, the congregation decided to appoint a new minister, the Rev. Harold Johnson. It was an act of faith. The membership had dwindled to almost nothing. The sensible thing seemed to be to sell the site.

But they didn't. Instead they asked Mr Johnson to be their minister. And one of his first ideas was to provide a thought for the week—not for the man in the pew, but for those passing the church. It would be printed on a poster in big, bold letters that could be seen easily in passing. It would be short and crisp. Every week it would be changed.

So, one Sunday just over 50 years ago, up went the first poster. It proclaimed the words, "Don't Worry—It May Never Happen."

It was, in fact, the first-ever "Wayside Pulpit" message. Now they appear on church noticeboards in every land—ten-second sermons holding out hope and promise. And if you walk down Cross Street today you'll see one outside the thriving church where it all started.

Thursday—October 4.

> *P*LEASE *be kind if you can;*
>   *You'll never regret it.*
> *But once you've been kindly,*
>   *Be quick to forget it.*
> *Don't tell me that people*
>   *Are kind to you never,*
> *But try to remember*
>   *Their kindness for ever!*

THE FRIENDSHIP BOOK

FRIDAY—OCTOBER 5.

IN New Kensington, Pennsylvania, you'll find the home of our good and cheerful friend, Dan Stewart.

Dan never writes a letter without enclosing a few thoughts or a story with a smile. I hope you like this, about the young Abraham Lincoln.

It seems Lincoln was walking to Springfield on a hot and dusty day when a carriage made up on him. Lincoln hailed the driver and asked if he'd mind taking his overcoat into town.

"With pleasure," said the stranger. "But how will you get your coat again?"

"Easily," smiled Lincoln. "I intend to stay in it!"

SATURDAY—OCTOBER 6.

SMILE if you like—but think about it, too.

One evening in a hotel a group of holiday-makers were having a friendly chat when a large and overbearing guest marched in, took up the topic which was being discussed at that moment, and held forth with tremendous emphasis, giving her own views and convictions, and going on and on and on till her sister came to see what was happening and thankfully relieved the group of the " terror."

In the blessed silence which followed, an old man, smiling a little, remarked in low tones, "Yes, there's a time for saying nothing and there's a time for saying something, but there's never a time for saying everything."

How true!

SUNDAY—OCTOBER 7.

BUT I have trusted in Thy mercy; my heart shall rejoice in Thy salvation.

THE FRIENDSHIP BOOK

Monday—October 8.

MURRAY SPANGLER was an engineer. Because of his cough he had to give up a good job. He became a janitor.

Not the best kind of job for a man afflicted with a cough, I'd have thought, and Murray soon found out, too. For as he swept the rooms and corridors he found his brush raised so much dust his cough became worse than ever. He knew he could never hold down his job if he didn't find an answer to the problem.

So he set to work. He took a length of hose, a wooden box and an old broom handle. Then he fitted a small electric motor to his contraption. And when he started it up and pushed it along the floor in front of him, hey presto, it sucked up the dust as he went!

It was the very first vacuum cleaner of all. Murray was so pleased with it he showed it to a friend whose name was Hoover. Together they decided that what it did for Murray it could do for thousands of housewives. So they set to work to refine the machine, and then put the new invention on the market.

The rest you know, except, perhaps, that Murray Spangler's invention came too late to cure his cough. He died from asthma while still quite a young man.

How strange that the very misfortune which took his life gave him the idea that has brought blessing to so many harassed housewives.

Tuesday—October 9.

JUST a thought for today:
Be content with what you have—but never with what you are.

THE FRIENDSHIP BOOK

Wednesday—October 10.

IT'S those who have not very much,
But share their little bit,
Who really find life well worth while
And get some fun from it.
They have the knack of getting by
Without a fuss—do you and I?

Thursday—October 11.

I NEVER met Bill Bosson.

He worked in a shoe factory in Stafford, and the very shoes I wear might well have been made by him.

His home was 3 Prospect Road, but you'd seldom find him there. He'd be away helping someone—giving a neighbour a hand to repair his car, putting a new plug on an old body's electric fire, and so on. It didn't matter what it was—Bill was the chap to put it right.

Then one day Bill felt a pain . . . and the verdict was cancer. It was just a matter of time. Yet Bill simply squared his shoulders, forced himself to smile, and carried on as before. When anyone asked how he was he smiled again and said, " I'm all right."

Of course he wasn't. Yet only days before he died in hospital at 44, when his sister asked him if he was " all right," he managed to grin and nod.

To me, the most remarkable tribute to Bill is that the day after he went into hospital the ward sister had no fewer than 26 phone calls about him before 11 a.m. Even more remarkable is that all the calls were from friends his relatives never knew he had.

As I say, I never met Bill Bosson. But I feel I know him.

THE FRIENDSHIP BOOK

FRIDAY—OCTOBER 12.

IT sounds remarkable.

But a friend of mine who knows about such things assures me it's perfectly true. He dropped in the other evening just as the Lady of the House had finished planting some bulbs. As she was clearing up, he said to me, " It has nothing to do with bulbs, Francis, but did you know that if you planted a single grain of wheat today and allowed it to flourish unchecked, it would take only eight years for that grain to feed everyone on this earth for twelve months?"

Amazing, indeed—and isn't it the same if you plant a careless word, or a kindly thought?

SATURDAY—OCTOBER 13.

AT Auchinleck Academy in Ayrshire, the senior girls put their cooking lessons to good use.

Once they've prepared a meal in the school they take it to the home of a pensioner. There they set the table, serve the food, and sit down for a chat.

It's a lovely idea. Yet, would you believe it, the Lady of the House and I had quite a discussion about it. The question is—who gains most from this? The girls, being led into womanhood along the paths of consideration for others? Or the old folk, enjoying a meal they haven't had to cook themselves, in the company of a lively young lass?

I suspect, however, the Lady of the House has the kernel of it. She affirms that a dinner is done in half an hour. But some of the wisdom and commonsense the old people have gathered over a lifetime will surely rub off on to the girls, standing them in good stead in the days that lie ahead of them.

And that, you might say, is the bonus of a good deed well done.

THE FRIENDSHIP BOOK

SUNDAY—OCTOBER 14.

WHO can say, I have made my heart clean, I am pure from my sin?

MONDAY—OCTOBER 15.

ONE of the hardest tasks a widow must face is to go through her husband's belongings after his death.

Several months passed before Mrs Helen Clewlow, of Stoke, could bring herself to do so.

She was about to discard one of his jackets when she felt a piece of paper in the pocket. It was headed in her husband's handwriting with the date of their marriage—April 25, 1925.

As she read on, her eyes filled with tears, for she found it was a message, "To my dear wife, Helen":

My home you entered, there to be a light,
Shining within when all without is night.
My guardian angel, o'er my life presiding,
Doubling my pleasures, and my cares dividing.

Can you think of a lovelier tribute from a husband to his wife? I found myself wondering why Mr Clewlow had it in his pocket. Had he kept it there knowing that one day, after he had gone, his wife would find it and perhaps gain comfort and strength?

No one will ever know. But for Mrs Clewlow these simple lines have become her most precious keepsake of 46 happy years.

TUESDAY—OCTOBER 16.

NOW if you say you'll do a thing,
  Don't shout ere it's begun;
Leave shouting to the folk who see—
What you attempted DONE!

THE FRIENDSHIP BOOK

WEDNESDAY—OCTOBER 17.

NOBODY'S perfect, we all know that. But sometimes we need to be reminded of that fact—as this new version of an old saying does so well!

There's so much good in the worst of us,
So much bad in the best of us,
That it's hard to tell which one of us
Ought to reform the rest of us!

THURSDAY—OCTOBER 18.

A FRIEND of mine was driving from Johnstone to Kilbirnie, in the West of Scotland. Suddenly he came on a young man bowling merrily down the road—in a wheel-chair! Not a mechanical one, either, but one propelled by rims on the wheels.

My friend stopped to ask if help was needed. But no, everything was fine. Matt McDonald was the man pushing himself along in the wheelchair. He was 27, and four years before, had been paralysed in a car accident.

Matt had wakened to a beautiful morning. It was cold, certainly. But the sky was blue. What a grand day, thought Matt, to have a run down to Kilbirnie—15 miles away!

He didn't tell a soul he was going. He wheeled himself out of the house after breakfast, waved good-bye to his mother, and set off. It was tough going some of the way, but the harder it got the more Matt was determined not to give in. He covered almost the whole 15 miles before another car drew up, and out jumped his father, worried stiff in case Matt had come to grief.

I've heard many a story of courage. But Matt McDonald and his magnificent miles in a wheelchair in their way take a lot of beating.

THE FRIENDSHIP BOOK

FRIDAY—OCTOBER 19.

MY friend, John Bunney, of 25 Laburnum Avenue, Consett, sent me this story.

A little girl was taken to church for the first time. When the minister said, " Let us pray," each member of the congregation bowed his head. The girl looked round, mystified to see everyone apparently staring intently at the floor.

" Mummy," she said in a loud, clear voice, " what are we all looking for?"

Of course, there were broad smiles from everyone there. But one or two left the service that day wondering about the child's simple question.

When you pray, what do *you* look for?

SATURDAY—OCTOBER 20.

SOME people have a happy knack of finding a sermon or a challenging thought anywhere and at any time. Martin Luther was one of them, as this quotation written centuries ago very clearly shows :

" I have one preacher I love better than any other. He is my tame robin, who preaches to me every day. After he has taken his crumbs he hops to a tree close by my door, lifts up his voice to God, singing his carols of praise and gratitude. Then he tucks his head under his wing and goes to sleep, leaving tomorrow to look after itself."

In these anxious days, would not some of us do well to trust more and worry less?

SUNDAY—OCTOBER 21.

IF ye keep my commandments, ye shall abide in my love; even as I have kept my Father's commandments, and abide in his love.

THE FRIENDSHIP BOOK

Monday—October 22.

I UNDERSTAND the smallest Japanese coin is one yen.

It is worth so little that anyone who drops a yen in a busy street doesn't bother to pick it up.

It's difficult to gather between finger and thumb, and the reward is scarcely worth the effort.

But these little coins are picked up, for all that, because women in the Salvation Army of Japan are always on the lookout for them. They do wonderful work with them—feeding the hungry, clothing the orphan, caring for the old and sick. What's more, these despised coins brought 39 poor Salvationists in Japan from their home on a lonely island to an important meeting at their headquarters.

It's always dangerous to say anything is worthless. Somebody may find a use for what seems unusable, just as some power can take the most unpromising people and make heroes and saints of them!

Tuesday—October 23.

IN the porch of an American church there is, I understand, a notice which reads:

" Enter To Worship : Depart To Serve."

That does seem to me to sum up a great deal of what religion is about. We do well to realise that we attend a service for the good of our own souls so that by worship our spirits are cleansed and made strong again through God's grace.

This is indeed good for us and a joy in itself ; but after worship comes the challenge to serve others, help the needy, to share a burden. The world has never before needed more desperately all dedicated men and women whose religion comprises worship and service.

THE FRIENDSHIP BOOK

WEDNESDAY—OCTOBER 24.

I AM indebted to Mr William Edwards, of Shrewsbury, for these brave lines:
*Count your garden by the flowers,
   Never by the leaves that fall;
Count your joys by golden hours,
   Never when life's worries call.
Count your nights by stars, not shadows,
   Count your days by smiles, not tears;
And when life's span so swiftly narrows,
   Count your age by friends, not years.*

THURSDAY—OCTOBER 25.

THIS is the story of an old Highland shepherd who met a professor of botany on the hills.

They got talking, of course. Then the professor stooped and plucked a little flower at his feet and handed it and a magnifying glass to the shepherd. For a long moment the old man examined the flower. Then in an awed voice he said, " Man, tae think I've been stepping down wee bits of loveliness like this all my days!"

Perhaps you smile. But do you go through life missing much of what is lovely and of good report simply because you never think of looking?

FRIDAY—OCTOBER 26.

HOW your day ends depends to some extent on how you begin it.

I have a feeling that all of us might emulate a friend of mine who writes to tell me:
*I never go forth to meet a new day
Without asking God as I kneel down to pray
To give me the strength and courage to be
As patient with others as He is with me!*

THE FRIENDSHIP BOOK

SATURDAY—OCTOBER 27.

THIS story's about a pensioner who went to her doctor with a pain in her left leg. "It's awful sore, doctor," she said. "It keeps me off my sleep."

The doctor examined her carefully, then shook his head sadly. "I'm sorry, Maggie," he said, "but there's not much I can do. It's just old age."

"It can't be that, doctor," said Maggie, firmly. "The other leg's just as old. But it's not sore!"

SUNDAY—OCTOBER 28.

HE giveth power to the faint and to them that hath no might—He increaseth their strength.

MONDAY—OCTOBER 29.

IN one of her books, Elizabeth Byrd tells how she spent a stormy winter night in a cottage on a bleak slope among lonely hills in Scotland.

She and her hostess, Mrs MacIntosh, ate by candlelight. When the wind howled over the one chimney and the rain poured from an impenetrable black sky, there came a knock at the door and a neighbour's crippled son came limping in, soaked to the skin. He had been sent by his mother to ask if Mrs MacIntosh was all right, and was surprised to find she had a visitor.

As an exceptionally fierce gust shook the shutters, the laddie looked curiously at Elizabeth Byrd and asked if she were frightened.

"Of course, she was scared before you came," replied Mrs MacIntosh instantly. "But it's different now we've a man about."

Some folk have the gift for saying things like that—things that make even a cripple feel strong and active, even a small boy feel important.

THE FRIENDSHIP BOOK

TUESDAY—OCTOBER 30.

ONE July day, Mrs Hayhurst, of Slade Lane, Manchester, slipped into her church during the lunch hour for a few moments of quiet prayer.

Inside, her eyes were drawn to a beautiful array of white carnations, each one a perfect bloom. There was a card on the flowers, and Mrs Hayhurst found herself going softly forward to read the words on it.

All it said was:

In memory of Joy Veronica,
married here July 18.
Today would have been our silver wedding.

Deeply touched, Mrs Hayhurst stood very still, while the flowers seemed to shed a peace all around her. In the silence she tried to picture the husband who returned to the church where he had been married, bringing with him an armful of carnations. She saw him carefully arranging them, thinking as he did so, surely, of that day exactly 25 years before, when he had stood there as a young bridegroom with his chosen wife by his side, wondering what life had in store for them.

Now his bride of that day had gone, but he had never forgotten her. And on his lonely pilgrimage back to the church they were married in, he wrote the three short lines which spoke of a love that had never faded.

WEDNESDAY—OCTOBER 31.

IF only all the world could learn
  The simple art of living,
They'd know that each was born to fill
  His daily life in giving.
For only those who love to give
  Have ever really learnt to live!

NOVEMBER

Thursday—November 1.

WHEN Toscanini was in his teens he played the cello in a small orchestra in Italy. His sight was poor. He couldn't afford spectacles. In the orchestra, the music stand was too far away for him to read the printed notes. So, in his spare time, Toscanini spent hours memorising not only his part, but the music played by every other instrument, so he'd know when to come in.

Then one evening, just before an important concert, the conductor fell ill. Toscanini, just 19, was the only musician who knew the whole programme by heart. So he was called on to conduct the orchestra, and he did so without a note of music in front of him.

The audience gave him a standing ovation—so much so that Toscanini, the unknown cellist in a minor orchestra, was launched on the road that was to make him one of the most famous conductors who has ever lived. So, in a way, the misfortune of Toscanini's poor sight turned out to be perhaps the greatest stroke of luck in his life.

Worth remembering, when things seem to be against you.

Friday—November 2.

IT'S a fine way to live, the code contained in this little rhyme :
It's giving and doing for somebody else—
On that all life's splendour depends.
And all the sweet joys of this wonderful world
Are found in the keeping of friends!

THE FRIENDSHIP BOOK

SATURDAY—NOVEMBER 3.

ONE afternoon when I was driving through a little town I caught sight of a few words printed in large letters on a wayside pulpit. I had no need to pull up. I did not slow down. I read the six words in a flash, but I thought about them for days and feel that they are a challenge to me every hour of every day.

The six words are: *He stands best who kneels most.*

SUNDAY—NOVEMBER 4.

FOR Thou hast been a strength to the poor, a strength to the needy in his distress, a refuge from the storm.

MONDAY—NOVEMBER 5.

IT will be only older readers who remember the days of Annie S. Swan, who was born near Edinburgh in 1860, and died in 1943. For long years she wrote gracious and lovable stories, and her serials were eagerly followed week by week. She was, indeed, one of the most popular writers of her day.

She loved all things good and beautiful, and found the best in the men and women she met. She was kindness itself, and always truthful—always except once, she tells us in one of her books. That was when she was five. She went to play in a hayfield, and on the way home a new hat she was wearing got lost in a load of hay. When her mother asked what happened, Annie said she didn't know—*she hadn't worn the hat out of doors.* Of course, that was an out and out lie—but she was scared.

What interests me is that over 70 years later she remembered the trifling incident, *and regretted it.*

THE FRIENDSHIP BOOK

TUESDAY—NOVEMBER 6.

I MET a quaint old gentleman
  One foggy winter's day.
Said he to me right merrily:
  "Friend, spring is on the way!"
"Poor chap," said I, "his mind has gone . . ."
  But when I'd thought a while
I realised how right he was—
  And simply had to smile.
The days ahead may cheerless be,
  But spring is coming—just you see!

WEDNESDAY—NOVEMBER 7.

AS a rule, I'm not in favour of parodies. But there are exceptions to every rule, and I cannot help liking this story about the lady who was in hospital recovering from a serious throat operation.

Sadly, she was not making very good progress because she was so afraid to swallow. Try as she would, she couldn't take the plunge, and she did so want to do as the kind nurses urged.

Come Sunday, a group of evangelists came round the wards with a short service, and one of their choruses began, " My Lord knows the way through the wilderness, all I have to do is follow." By the time the singers left, our lady had the answer to her problem, and before each meal was due she earnestly prayed her little parody:

My Lord knows the way through the wilderness,
All I have to do is SWALLOW!
Strength for today is mine alway,
And all I need for tomorrow,
My Lord knows the way through the wilderness,
All I have to do is SWALLOW!

Need I add that she did!

THE FRIENDSHIP BOOK

Thursday—November 8.

As the British Legion's Festival of Remembrance nears its end, all is silence. A lone bugler sounds the Last Post. Then, as the last ringing note echoes away, a million poppy petals begin to float down from the roof, only a few at first, but soon swirling down like a scarlet snowfall. It is an unforgettable sight, shared by millions on TV.

Far above the heads of the audience the lone figure of a rigger climbs hundreds of steps to the dome of the hall. There, in the darkness, beyond the glare of the floodlights, he waits for the final note of the Last Post to release the nets holding the poppy petals. Beside him are stacked boxes full of more petals, specially dampened to make them fall steadily. Throughout the two minutes' silence he casts them out into the darkness, one for each of the 1,534,415 who fell in two world wars.

I cannot help thinking how right it is that an unknown workman, a humble man in a humble job, should be entrusted with the task of releasing the scarlet snowfall that honours all those humble men who scaled the very heights of heroism.

Friday—November 9.

Years ago someone who was rather liverish remarked: "The young have aspirations that never come to pass; the old have reminiscences of what never happened."

Well, I dare say it is true. I'm not denying it. All I can say is that life is not a bed of roses but most of it is fairly comfortable, the sun shines, kindnesses are done, we miss one star and hit another, and we look back, quite forgetting the bad weather and remembering mostly happy days gone by. I don't think we can ask for much more.

THE FRIENDSHIP BOOK

SATURDAY—NOVEMBER 10.

TIME and time again I remark that truth is stranger than fiction, and so, indeed, it is. Not even Charles Dickens dared to make Scrooge as miserably close-fisted as he could, because, had he done so, nobody would have believed him.

But Hetty Green was fact. She died in 1916, leaving over 95,000,000 dollars, say twenty million pounds in British currency—and that at a time when money bought at least three times as much as it does today, so that we can think of Hetty being worth as much as sixty millionaires!

And how did Hetty live? Like the poorest beggar on the streets. *She ate her porridge cold because she begrudged the cost of heating it!*

But she wasn't born that way. Greed shaped her! How sad.

SUNDAY—NOVEMBER 11.

WHEN thou wast weary with the length of the way thou didst not say "There is no hope," but there did come a quickening of thy strength; therefore thou didst not faint.

MONDAY—NOVEMBER 12.

AT lunch-time the Lady of the House gave me a letter to post.

"It'll need a stamp," she told me. Knowing there was a stamp in the letter rack, I said, "No, there's one in the stamp book we can use."

"Oh, but I can't use that," says she. Naturally, I asked why not.

"Because," she replied, "it might be needed!"

There's no getting past the logic of women.

THE FRIENDSHIP BOOK

TUESDAY—NOVEMBER 13.

EVER been to Abbotsinch Airport? Alex Panton has.

Behind that apparently simple statement lies a story of courage, sheer determination and love. Alex is 62, and a crippling illness has kept him in bed, unable even to sit up, for over 30 years.

On the rare occasions when he is taken out, he must be pushed, lying flat out, on a kind of trolley. So, when he said to his wife he'd like to see the airport, he never really thought he'd ever get there. But Mrs Panton made up her mind that, for once, Alex wouldn't be disappointed. So on a fine afternoon she lifted him on to his trolley, tucked him up warmly and set off for Abbotsinch and back—a round trip of over 10 miles.

Oh, they took a wrong turning and went the long way round. And they were caught in a rainstorm. But doggedly Mrs Panton carried on until, with some friendly help, they reached the airport.

What a thrill for Alex. And just as big a thrill for his wife to see him enjoying himself. Then came the long trek home again, and by the time they got there, Mrs Panton had pushed Alex nearly 15 miles.

In a way, that journey's like Alex's life—a difficult road, some clouds ; but, because of the blessing of a loving wife, so much sunshine, too.

WEDNESDAY—NOVEMBER 14.

IT'S when your heart is sad and sore,
  When life seems cold and grim,
That courage ebbs and faith is small,
  Your lonely road most dim.
Pray then that you may surely find
An inward strength, a quiet mind.

THE FRIENDSHIP BOOK

Thursday—November 15.

THERE'S nothing easier to make than an excuse.
Whether that excuse will stand up to a good hard look is, of course, another matter. Especially when you measure it against the faithfulness and courage of someone like Greta Stewart.

Twice a week Greta visits her sister, Jean, in hospital, and she's been making the journey now for more than 20 years.

Her neighbours see her leaving the house where she lives alone, every Wednesday and Saturday with her little brown case. But Greta doesn't see them for she's blind. Nevertheless, she takes the bus into town, makes her way to the station and gets on the train. Then, after her visit to Jean, she makes the same journey back again—a round trip of thirty miles.

Oh, I dare say it would be easy enough for Greta to tell herself she doesn't really have to go so often, especially when the pavements are slippery with frost, or when it's raining. But that isn't her way. She knows Jean's expecting her, and that's enough for her.

Did I say excuses are easy to make? I've a feeling that, once you know the story of Greta Stewart they don't seem so easy after all.

Friday—November 16.

IF you can say a friendly word,
Or give a bit of cheer;
If you can help some needy friend
When tragedy seems near;
If you can share somebody's grief
While clouds black out the sun,
You're doing something, you'll agree,
Which needed to be done.

TOP PEOPLE

*Get to the top of the tree you may
And know the joy of winning,
But, brother, when you try to stay,
The fun is just beginning!*

DAVID HOPE

A QUIET BAY

Round the hills the clouds may pour,
Foam may lace the bay;
Lonely on the curving shore
I would wish to stray.

*Braving Nature's every mood,
One with wind and waves,
Finding in her solitude
What the spirit craves.*

DAVID HOPE

OUR POSTMAN

You could call him a cog in a national wheel,
  A link in a very long chain;
It would be true, but it wouldn't be just
  For it wouldn't be making it plain
That whatever the weather, he always gets through
  Going that extra mile,
To keep us in touch with the world outside
  With a letter, a word and a smile.

DAVID HOPE

THE FRIENDSHIP BOOK

SATURDAY—NOVEMBER 17.

AS a rule Miss Alison knocks at the door, comes in, and says happily to the Lady of the House, " It's me !"

Then she arranges a small chair and a stool in a corner of the kitchen, sits herself comfortably in the chair and places William Henry on the stool—William Henry, I should add, is a teddy bear.

Once Miss Alison has a plate of crisps she chats away, and once she noted that my wife had a pile of washing-up. " If I were you, Mrs Gay," she remarked, " I should finish paring the potatoes and then get on with the washing-up." And added, " *You'll be so glad when it's done!*"

I don't know many philosophers under five !

SUNDAY—NOVEMBER 18.

MARK the perfect man, and behold the upright: for the end of that man is peace.

MONDAY—NOVEMBER 19.

THESE lines came all the way from Miss Lily Barber in New Zealand:
Build a little homely house
  And fence it round about
With quietness and happiness
  To keep the troubles out.
All the walls are thankfulness,
  And all the planks are prayer,
And faith and trust keep off the rust
  That comes of anxious care.
Hope's the roof that shelters you
  From every wind of wrong,
And loves own light on the hearth burns bright
  To warm you all day long.

THE FRIENDSHIP BOOK

Tuesday—November 20.

I WONDER if you know that this very wonderful prayer was first sung by monks at Old Sarum, in Wiltshire, nearly 800 years ago.

God be in my head
And in my understanding.
God be in my eyes
And in my looking.
God be in my mouth
And in my speaking.
God be in my heart
And in my thinking.
God be at mine end
And at my departing.

For me, it says everything.

Wednesday—November 21.

I OVERHEARD two very modern misses on the bus discussing the different forms of the marriage service.

The discussion got very heated, I may say, as one of the ladies, who was certainly no supporter of Women's Lib, argued that she wanted to love, honour and *obey*. For, she said, if you really loved someone, you would be only too happy to obey them, and, anyway, shouldn't the husband be the boss? Her friend, however, was more in favour of loving, honouring and cherishing.

Intrigued, I looked up the exact meaning of both words in the dictionary when I got home. It said:

Cherish.—To protect and treat with affection: to nurture, nurse: to entertain in the mind.

Obey.—To render obedience: to do what one is told: to be governed or controlled: to comply with.

Well, for my part, I think I'd rather be cherished than obeyed. What about you?

THE FRIENDSHIP BOOK

Thursday—November 22.

*When looking back I wonder how
I kept on keeping on.
The years were harsh, the money scarce,
Sometimes all strength seemed gone.
But somehow, well, I struggled through—
And surely you will do so, too!*

Friday—November 23.

It's many years now since Bob O'Haire came over from Ireland as a lad of 17, with no education and half a crown in his pocket. The first thing he did when he landed was to slip into a church for a few minutes. Then he went out to find a job as a labourer.

He fought in the First World War, and he received a wound which plagued him all his days. But he kept on working, and every day he went to church, sometimes twice. He would rise at six in the morning simply to spend a little time there, and on his way home from work he would call in again.

As he grew older and couldn't walk up the hill to his own church, Bob took the bus to the middle of Glasgow every day, and got off at a stop beside a church. And not long ago, when he had a stroke and two heart attacks he and his wife moved to a ground-floor flat just across the street from yet another church so Bob could still get across for his daily visit.

And it was there that Bob, the faithful old labourer, was called home. He died in church, kneeling in prayer, aged 79.

Bob never preached. He practised—a man who, through thick and thin, stood by his faith to the end.

THE FRIENDSHIP BOOK

SATURDAY—NOVEMBER 24.

HERE is a hint on the art of keeping peace in the home.

The story was told by a farmer to a holidaymaker. "Ay," said the farmer in answer to a query, "I'm married, happily married, and have four youngsters to be proud of. I can honestly say that in twenty-five years me and my wife have never had a quarrel."

The holidaymaker, duly impressed, inquired how the farmer had contrived to live so happily. "Well," was the reply, "from the very beginning, my wife and I had an understanding that every morning she was free to do as she pleased ; and then, for the rest of the day I was free to do anything she wanted."

Merely a laugh? Perhaps so. I'm not quite sure.

SUNDAY—NOVEMBER 25.

WAIT on the Lord; be of good courage, and He shall strengthen thine heart.

MONDAY—NOVEMBER 26.

IN these days when so many people are content to do the "done thing," without ever giving much thought to reasons or consequences, we might take a hint from a Russian proverb which says : *To live your life is not as simple as crossing a field.*

Life is short, and to make a success of it requires some thought. Hoping it will all work out for the best is hardly enough. All of which is a good reason or excuse for now and then sitting alone with yourself and doing a bit of looking back and some forward planning.

THE FRIENDSHIP BOOK

TUESDAY—NOVEMBER 27.

THE besetting sin of an Irish teenager was pride in her very striking good looks. She dressed herself to look as attractive as possible—and who's to blame her for that? And if she arrived at church a minute late so that the congregation might take an admiring look at her, why, that was hardly criminal.

One day, however, she summoned up enough humility to confess her pride to the priest. "It's my vanity, Father," she declared, perhaps feeling virtuous as she made the confession. "It's my beauty."

The kindly old priest may have chuckled to himself—we do not know; but the colleen was taken aback when he said gently, "Sure, my dear, that's no sin at all, at all. It's a delusion."

WEDNESDAY—NOVEMBER 28.

THESE lines, sent me by Robert Rawlinson, who lives near Stockport, are inscribed in stone on the doorway of the Rutland Arms Hotel, an old coaching inn at Bakewell, Derbyshire:

Here's to one who took his chances in a busy world of men, battled luck and circumstances, fought and fell and fought again. Won sometimes, but did no crowing, lost sometimes, but did not wail; took his beating but kept going, never let his courage fail. He was fallible and human, therefore loved and understood both his fellow man and woman, whether good or not so good. Kept his spirit undiminished, never let down any friend; played the game till it was finished, lived a sportsman to the end.

No one seems to know today, even at the hotel, whom the lines remember. But any man would feel honoured to have them written about him.

THE FRIENDSHIP BOOK

Thursday—November 29.

WHAT advice can we give our youngsters setting out on their working lives? Not much, really, but we could do worse than the father at the station seeing his lad off to take up a job in London.

He knew the boy was ambitious, so, before he waved good-bye, the father (not often very serious) added a few words of wisdom. " Well, Tom," he said. " We'll be proud to see you doing well— you know that. But bear in mind that it's a good thing to be nice to folk on your way up—you might meet them again on your way down!"

Friday—November 30.

THE Lady of the House and I often think of this letter which came to me from a woman in Ayrshire who had been recently widowed and I'd like to share it with you.

" Dear Francis," the letter read, " my husband died recently. He was a gentle, kind man, who loved his family, and, being a young-at-heart grandpa, delighted in playing with his grandchildren. During the last five weeks of his life our daughter and grandchildren, aged 3 and $1\frac{1}{2}$, visited him each week-end. But by that time, alas, he could no longer enjoy their company.

" Before he became ill they were always too busy to come, though only an hour's run away. After it was all over, I found on his bedside table a little poem he had written. It contained this line: ' Hast not a little time to spare, to care with thought, for those who cared for thee?' "

No self-pity. But a message for all of us, who, being human, take our loved ones for granted.

DECEMBER

SATURDAY—DECEMBER 1.

THOSE of you who have been inside Westminster Abbey will probably remember it much as I do.

The striking beauty of the soaring stone columns, with sunlight filtering through stained glass to fall gently on the tomb of the Unknown Soldier. The memorials to great men. Perhaps you even feel a quiet pride as people of all colours and creeds walk round drinking in the centuries of our history.

Yet I wonder if you know the most magnificent time of day in the Abbey is one o'clock. On the stroke of that hour, every day, a voice can be heard saying quietly from concealed loudspeakers, " Please, would you all stand still?" And, a little surprised, people will stop in their tracks as the voice goes on to say, " Every day in this beautiful Abbey at one o'clock we say the Lord's Prayer."

Then stillness descends, heads bow, and here and there can be heard the whispered, immemorial prayer, " Our Father . . ."

To me, the most splendid part is that it commemorates no moment of history, no great man, no national escape, but it is said simply as part of the daily worship in Westminster Abbey— a reminder that the heart of our nation is still sound.

SUNDAY—DECEMBER 2.

AND thou, Bethlehem, in the land of Judah, art not least among the Princes of Judah: for out of thee shall come a Governor that shall rule my people Israel.

THE FRIENDSHIP BOOK

MONDAY—DECEMBER 3.

BIRKET FOSTER, the artist, told this story of the time he spent with Tennyson shortly before the poet died.

On the last walk they had together, as they were going through a dark clump of trees, Tennyson said, "Does it not seem to you, as a landscape painter, that going through an avenue of trees with light beyond, is like passing through the grave to eternity?"

At this season, when evening shadows and chills increase, the parable is impressive . . . beyond every night is the dawn.

TUESDAY—DECEMBER 4.

YOU'RE almost certain to know the story of the telegram sent to an elderly golf professional who was something of a bore.

Whoever sent the telegram was indeed a stickler for truth. His message to the pro, who was then on the sick-list, read, "*By a majority of seven to five, the committee wishes you a speedy recovery.*"

Speaking the truth is highly desirable, but, as a wise old Quaker once remarked, "You needn't *always* be speaking it!"

WEDNESDAY—DECEMBER 5.

NOW, happy folk are busy folk:
 They lend a willing hand;
They share a trouble or a joy—
 Somehow they understand.
They've just not time to grouse or sulk—
 They're wanted everywhere;
They're on their toes from morn till night,
 And serving is their prayer.

THE FRIENDSHIP BOOK

Thursday—December 6.

SHE was the greatest person alive in the world of her day—a queen, an empress, ruler of an enormous part of the world. She was Queen Victoria, and with a stroke of a pen she could change life for millions.

The last time she drove in state in London the vast crowds cheered and waved, for everybody was proud of the most famous Royal person in the world; but a man who raised his hat, murmured to his daughter, "There she goes poor little body . . . I think she'd be happier if she were your mother."

After all, it doesn't take much to make us happy.

Friday—December 7.

NO wonder Alec Gordon was excited!

He was to fly to Australia for a three-month holiday with his daughter. What an adventure for a retired railwayman of 74!

There was one snag. Alec, president of the local pensioners' club, would miss one of the highlights of the year—their Christmas party.

So his old friends put their heads together and decided the party wouldn't be the same without Alec, and they'd bring it forward by a month.

So the Christmas dinner was duly held early. There was a rousing cheer with the toast to wish Alec a safe journey and a happy holiday.

Alas, though no one there could ever have guessed it, there was to be no holiday for Alec. Less than a week later, on the eve of his departure, he collapsed and died.

His old friends were stunned and saddened. Yet, even in their sorrow, they give quiet thanks that, because of a Christmas dinner in November, Alec's last memories were also among his happiest.

THE FRIENDSHIP BOOK

SATURDAY—DECEMBER 8.

ONE of our friends is an intrepid pioneer, who, in his more active years, has taken immense, if calculated, risks. One winter afternoon he rang up his daughter, who intended coming home that evening, telling her not to set off by car, explaining the fog was gathering.

His daughter laughed. "You!" she exclaimed. "Goodness, *you've* never been cautious!"

"Oh, yes, I have," was the serious reply. "Sometimes you have to take risks. But when you *can* stay put and be safe, it's common-sense to do so."

Then he rang off. I think he did the right thing. Do you?

SUNDAY—DECEMBER 9.

AND she shall bring forth a son, and thou shalt call His name Jesus.

MONDAY—DECEMBER 10.

SOME years ago a Yorkshire lassie set off for school with a jar of tadpoles. Unfortunately she slipped, the jar broke, and her right hand was very badly cut. The deep wound healed, but for all that, the doctors were grave. They said she might lose control of the muscles of her fingers.

Well, that was a trouble indeed. As it happened, somebody suggested that the lassie learn to play an accordion. So the patient did. She took lessons. She practised night and day, and, indeed, did so well that within months she was Yorkshire's top accordionist!

So the worst turned best for the Yorkshire lassie—but only because she made up her mind to do something . . . *and did it!*

THE FRIENDSHIP BOOK

TUESDAY—DECEMBER 11.

THIS old carol has the true Christmas spirit:—
*This time of the year is spent in good cheer,
And neighbours together do meet,
To sit by the fire, with friendly desire,
Each other in love to greet.
Old grudges forgot are put in the pot,
All sorrows aside they lay;
The old and the young doth carol a song,
To drive the cold winter away.*

WEDNESDAY—DECEMBER 12.

THIS story happened while Sir Winston Churchill was staying at the palace in Copenhagen, guest of the Royal Family. He had taken his own batman with him to Denmark, and the man, forgetting Sir Winston had asked for a bowl of soup before he went to bed, had gone out.

A servant from the palace was sent to fetch him. The palace, it seemed, was in an uproar. What had happened to Sir Winston's soup? With sinking heart the man dashed back, and ran up the stairs to Churchill's room. Too late. He arrived just in time to see someone else carrying a bowl of soup through Sir Winston's door—none other than the King of Denmark!

It seems that when King Frederik heard the commotion he went to the kitchen, personally ladled out a generous helping, then set a tray and served the soup to Churchill himself.

When he died last year the people of Denmark felt they were saying farewell not only to their King, but to a friend. Surely that was because he was great enough to serve, in the humblest ways, those who stayed beneath his roof or lived within the land over which he ruled.

THE FRIENDSHIP BOOK

Thursday—December 13.

MY goodness, how the assistant in the shoe shop talked while fitting me with one pair after another. He was patience personified, and, eventually, I settled for a pair of brown shoes. I paid for them, and he presented me with a box neatly wrapped in brown paper, and I set off for home. But I turned back. " Excuse me," I said to the young assistant, " this parcel feels light !"

" Not surprising," was the reply. " The shoes are on the counter !"

It made my day . . . so comforting to know that other people slip up now and then !

Friday—December 14.

FOR weeks now the Lady of the House has been searching the shops for her Christmas cards. How much thought she puts into finding the right card for the right person. Auntie Bess likes dogs, and Uncle John collects the Old Master reproductions.

I'm sure she gets as much pleasure out of choosing them as in getting the lovely cards her friends send her ! And what a splendid selection there is to choose from. No, there will be no " Mr and Mrs Blank are not sending cards this year, but wish all their friends a happy Christmas and a prosperous New Year," for the Gays.

I often wonder, how do people who know Mr and Mrs Blank decide whether or not they are included in the good wishes to anonymous friends? And if you're alone at Christmas and getting on a bit, a notice in the paper, which may or may not include you, isn't much comfort, is it?

You may not agree with me, but I can't help feeling that just a little message to show that you're remembered means so much more.

THE FRIENDSHIP BOOK

SATURDAY—DECEMBER 15.

ONE Christmas Eve, in the early days of the Second World War, an English soldier set out for a French pillbox, farther down the Allied lines. From a distance it seemed to be illuminated by something, and as he got nearer he was amazed to see that on top of the pillbox was a typical German Christmas tree, all lit up.

The Germans themselves were only a short distance away, across no-man's-land.

"Aren't you afraid they'll fire?" he asked the French officer who came to meet him.

"No, I don't think so," the Frenchman replied, smiling. "You see, we exchanged it for a turkey under a flag of truce."

SUNDAY—DECEMBER 16.

AND she brought forth her first born son, and wrapped Him in swaddling clothes, and laid Him in a manger.

MONDAY—DECEMBER 17.

THIS isn't the best season of the year—days can be dull and chilly, nights can be long to folk who are unable to go out, and it is so easy around this time to become just a bit sorry for oneself.

These thoughts came to me one drab day recently when I saw a wayside pulpit with the challenging message: *The Lord loveth a cheerful giver, and also a giver of cheer.*

That struck me as timely. It reminded me that however I may feel, it's my duty to be as friendly and good-humoured as I can, not just for the sake of Francis Gay, but in order to make life just the least bit brighter for others.

TUESDAY—DECEMBER 18.

DR NORMAN MACLEAN was walking with a forester friend one day when the conversation turned to evolution, which, for the forester, had replaced belief in God and the Creation.

Said Dr Maclean, "You believe that all the beauty and verdure you can see came by evolution; but the question is, how did evolution come?"

"By accident, so they say," was the reply.

"Accident!" said Dr Maclean. "In the year 1863 two great scientists, Lord Kelvin and Baron Liebig, were walking in the country and came to a glorious view like this. 'Do you believe,' asked Lord Kelvin, 'that the grass and flowers which we see around us grew by mere chemical forces?'

"'No,' answered Baron Liebig, 'no more than I could believe that a book of botany describing them could grow by mere chemical forces.'"

Then Dr Maclean said, "If you came upon a book describing your conifers and all the trees in the glen, you wouldn't believe the book grew up by accident."

"No," said the forester, "a book requires a thinker behind it."

"So does evolution," Dr Maclean concluded, "and the thinker's name is God."

WEDNESDAY—DECEMBER 19.

"*HOW could I tell?*" *the innkeeper asked.*
    "*How could I have known 'twas He?*
There were just a carpenter and his wife
    Come up from Galilee.
I would have bade them enter,
    And found them food and wine;
If only they'd explained to me,
If only there'd been a sign . . ."

THE FRIENDSHIP BOOK

THURSDAY—DECEMBER 20.

I WOULD like to pay tribute to Micky. Micky was a black Labrador who lived with Irene Mackenzie at Bolton in Lancashire.

He was a marvellous friend to Irene after she came out of hospital following her first eye operation. From the first, Micky was Irene's constant companion, and for 15 years he never failed to be her affectionate and wonderfully knowing friend and guide. Indoors or out, he seemed to understand every single word his mistress spoke. He was devoted to her ; and as the darkness closed around Irene he accompanied her everywhere, and delighted to lead her to the grocer's and the butcher's and the greengrocer's.

How he knew Thursday from any other day in the week remains a mystery even now, but as sure as Thursday arrived, he knew he and Irene would be off to the tripe shop, where he " paid " for one pound of tripe, and carried it home in a basket, never once trying to eat the delicacy he loved so much till he was home.

How can we explain the selfless service our animal friends so often give us?

FRIDAY—DECEMBER 21.

NOT long ago I had a letter from Mrs White of Dumbarton. In it she reminded me of a few lines I wrote many years ago. So here they are again, just a little reminder of where our duty lies, especially at this time of the year.

Your watchword now is—plot and plan,
Do all the secret good you can,
Take bairns and old folk by surprise,
And scatter stardust in their eyes . . .

I hope your stock of stardust is nearly ready !

THE FRIENDSHIP BOOK

SATURDAY—DECEMBER 22.

HARK the glad sound! the Saviour comes,
The Saviour promised long;
Let every heart exult with joy,
And every voice be song!

SUNDAY—DECEMBER 23.

GLORY to God in the highest, and on earth peace, goodwill toward men.

MONDAY—DECEMBER 24.

THE Barnes family had all gathered to share Christmas with the newest member, Ian, who had just celebrated his second birthday.

After the excitement of opening the parcels, it was time for the last door on the Advent calendar. "A baby s'eeping," announced Ian when the picture was revealed, and as he was told that the baby's name was Jesus there was a tiny prick of conscience in the family that this was the first time the Christ Child had been mentioned in the house that year; He had somehow been lost amidst the preparations.

Soon it was dinner-time, and once the candles were lit on the table, young Mrs Barnes called everyone through. Little Ian was the last to leave his toys, but as he rushed into the dining-room he stopped dead, then with a whoop, shouted, "Bir'day candles! Happy bir'day me?"

"No, pet," Mrs Barnes explained gently, lifting him up to the table. "It's the Baby Jesus's birthday."

There was a moment's pause, and then the little lad called down the table, "Sing, 'Happy bir'day, Jesus!'" And the family did just that.

How often it is a little child who leads us.

THE FRIENDSHIP BOOK

TUESDAY—DECEMBER 25.

N O shadows near to spoil your day,
 The family round your table;
The children opening up their gifts
 As fast as they are able.
Then spare a thought, where'er you are,
For those who know no Christmas star.

WEDNESDAY—DECEMBER 26.

"HE'S a brick!"

So said a nurse the other day to a little fellow, and I (who happened to be standing nearby), knew just what she meant: a gallant laddie who did as he was told, bore pain without flinching and could be relied upon.

Few people, I think, know how the expression came into common use. But there's a legend I'd like to retell for you.

Over three hundred years before Christ there was a king of Sparta named Agesilaus. That was when his kingdom was at the height of its glory. One day an ambassador was received by the king, who wished to impress his visitor, showing him round his capital —then the first city in Greece. At the end of the tour the ambassador remarked, " O, King, one thing in your capital astonishes me—you have no walls for defence, no great towers, no gates. Why is this?"

"Sir Ambassador," replied Agesilaus, "I fear you have not observed carefully. You shall tomorrow go with us and I will show you the walls of Sparta."

Next day the king drove with the ambassador out of the city to a plain where an army in battle-dress was drawn up in battle array. "Behold," said Agesilaus proudly, "the walls of Sparta — ten thousand men, and every man a brick!"

THE FRIENDSHIP BOOK

THURSDAY—DECEMBER 27.

THESE lines were written by an American soldier in Britain during the last war. Their message is just as true in the troubles we face today.

So long as there are homes where fires burn
  And there is bread;
So long as there are homes where lamps are lit
  And prayers are said;
Although a people falter through the dark
  And nations grope,
With God Himself back of these little homes
  We still can hope.

FRIDAY—DECEMBER 28.

CHRISTMAS is past. And some folk may feel that children these days are more than fortunate with so many lovely toys. As I write, my mind turns to Mrs Low, who's well past 80 now.

As little girls, she and her sister each possessed but one toy—a wooden doll. What tender care was taken of them! And on the day of their baby brother's christening, the two were allowed to take their dolls to church, if they promised to behave.

The minister, an understanding man, knew how proud the girls were of their dolls. So, after he'd christened the baby, he went forward and asked them if the dollies had a name. Then he led them both over to the font, and solemnly christened each doll!

There may be those who raise their eyebrows. But I think if they'd seen the stars in the eyes of two wee girls who carried their newly-christened dolls from the church, they would have realised, as the minister did, that whatever brings such joy to a child's heart deserves to be blessed.

And as for Mrs Low, to this day it is one of her most treasured memories.

THE FRIENDSHIP BOOK

SATURDAY—DECEMBER 29.

IT'S almost journey's end:
We're almost there,
And, looking back, the year has dealt me fair.
I had my worries,
But I'd laughter, too.
And happy days or sad, I saw them through.
What more can we expect?
What more should ask
Than strength to carry out life's daily task?

SUNDAY—DECEMBER 30.

LET us hear the conclusion of the whole matter: fear God, and keep His Commandments: for this is the whole duty of man.

MONDAY—DECEMBER 31.

WHEN the last minutes of the year are running out, friends of ours observe an old custom.

A few minutes before midnight the man of the house slips out. Then, as the strokes of twelve are sounding, he knocks at the door and hands his wife a small parcel.

It contains a piece of coal, salt and an old sixpenny piece.

Not very romantic, you may think! But that little parcel symbolises a great deal—a warm fireside, money to buy food and clothing, and salt to savour our food. In the old days, I suppose, the salt was indispensable for curing the barrel of herring we ate during the winter.

So the coal, the salt and the sixpence stand for all the material goods we really need.

May I wish you your share of them this New Year—and a little bit of jam on your bread, too!

Where the Photographs were taken

MEN OF THE SEA — *Hastings, Sussex.*

PEAT — *Lewis, Outer Hebrides.*

A SECRET BAY — *Blackpool Sands, Devon.*

DREAM COTTAGE — *By the River Exe at Bickleigh, Devon.*

NEWS! — *Ashton-Under-Hill, Worcestershire.*

WINDMILLS — *Denver Mill, Norfolk.*

A NEW DAY'S DAWNING — *Burford, in the valley af the River Windrush, Oxfordshire.*

ISLAND FORTRESS — *St Michael's Mount, Cornwall.*

ONCE IN A LIFETIME — *Loch Lomond at Balmaha, West Stirlingshire.*

TO CATCH A TROUT — *St John's Beck in the Vale of St John, Cumberland.*

DAYS IN THE PARK — *The grounds of the old Norman castle at Guildford, Surrey.*

RIVERSIDE — *Strand-on-the-Green, Middlesex.*

ON PARADE — *Crathie Church, Aberdeenshire.*

DECISIONS — *Beddgelert, on the borders of Caernarvonshire and Merioneth, North Wales.*

ADVENTURES — *Buckingham Palace.*

TOP PEOPLE — *Chester Zoo.*

A QUIET BAY — *Inch Strand, Co. Kerry, Eire.*

OUR POSTMAN — *Achlean, Glen Feshie, Inverness-shire.*

Printed and Published by D. C. THOMSON & CO., LTD.
12 Fetter Lane, Fleet Street, London, E.C.4.
© D. C. Thomson & Co., Ltd., 1972.